LES PORTES TORDUES

(THE TWISTED DOORS)

An Educational Bilingual Mystery

LES PORTES TORDUES
(THE TWISTED DOORS)
Bilingual French-English Edition

~~~~~~~~~~~~~~~~~~~~~~~~~~~~~~~~~~

Whoever heard of curling up on a nice,
soft, warm couch to actually enjoy
learning French?

The first chapters are a warm-up, but
you must learn them well *or else!*

Then, hang on tight to your pillow,
for this will be . . .

The Scariest Way in the World to Learn French!

~~~~~~~~~~~~~~~~~~~~~~~~~~~~~~~~~

Written and Conceived by
Dr. Kathie Dior
Formerly of the Université de Paris

Edited by
Servanne Woodward, Ph.D.
University of Western Ontario

~~DIOR PUBLISHING~~

For bulk rate pricing, ordering, and inquiries:
call Dior Publishing at 1-877-622-3176; visit
our website at www.thetwisteddoors.com; or
email us at info@thetwisteddoors.com

Graphics team: Krista Edmonds and Kathie Dior
Graphic artist: Krista Edmonds

Illustrations in chapters 4, 10, 13, 14, 29,
30, and 46 (figure 2) inspired by the original
Les portes tordues graphics: Andrew Edmonds

Audio CD direction: Kathie Dior
Audio CD narration: Lydie Guijarro
and Kathie Dior

A Spanish version is also available:
Las puertas retorcidas (The Twisted Doors):
The Scariest Way in the World to Learn Spanish! ™
ISBN-13: 978-0-9710227-2-0
ISBN-10: 0-9710227-2-0

Les portes tordues (The Twisted Doors):
The Scariest Way in the World to Learn French! ™
ISBN-13: 978-0-9710227-1-3
ISBN-10: 0-9710227-1-2

Printed in the United States of America

~~ TABLE DES MATIÈRES ~~

This book is dedicated to my son,
François, who brings me the joy of my life.
I hope that he will read this book to his future
children and grandchildren so that this book becomes a little
legacy for those progeny that I will not be here to meet and love.
I also wish to thank my beloved parents who taught me so many
things about life and gave me the splendid opportunity
to attend medical school in Paris, France.

~~ ACKNOWLEDGMENTS ~~

I wish to express my deepest gratitude to the native French-speaking editor, Servanne Woodward, Ph.D., University of Western Ontario, Canada, for masterfully editing this book. However, her greatest gift was her belief in me, without which, *The Twisted Doors* series would never have been written.

My sincere appreciation goes to Dr. Carole Edwards, native French speaker and Ph.D. in Francophone Studies from Purdue University and M.A. from the Université de Caen, France, for carefully reading this book in search of inaccuracies.

I would like to extend my special thanks to the graphic artist, Krista Edmonds of Edmonds Productions for her expertise and rare collaborative effort and patience, and to Andrew Edmonds for his remarkable illustrations inspired by the graphics found in the first version of *Les portes tordues*.

I wish to commend Lydia Guijarro, M.A., Université Stendhal (Grenoble), for her wonderfully dramatic interpretation of Françoise on the audio CD.

Lastly, I wish to thank the Purdue University Gifted Education Resource Institute (GERI), West Lafayette, Indiana, for having faith in using *Les portes tordues* as the French-language teaching tool for its students.

~~ PRÉFACE ~~

This book and its accompanying audio CD are meant to take you on a most unfamiliar journey into the world of French. Here are the directions for using the book itself: There are none . . . Well, maybe you need to know one thing: every line of the French story will always correspond to the same number line of the English translation. For instance, look at Chapitre 1. Look at line 2 of the French text. Now, logically speaking, which line of the English translation do you think will correspond to this line? If you said line 3, you had better send back this book! O.K. Those are the directions (or should I say "direction" with no "s" for the book). As for the audio CD, here are a few suggestions: Listen to it once as you follow the new French text. Then go back to the book and concentrate on learning the chapter. When you have passed the chapter test, listen to the CD again with the book open and then with the book *closed!* How many words or phrases can you now understand without peeking at the text? One last suggestion for the CD: For a zany subtitled effect that will skyrocket your acquisition of French intonation, listen to the CD as you follow the *English* text! Now, are you ready to begin? If so, just turn to page 1, pop in the audio CD, find a nice comfortable setting, sit down (unless you prefer standing), and start to read and listen. You will see how to proceed and what you are expected to do. One note: Don't skip anything. You'll see why later!

If you find yourself pulling out perfectly good hair because you don't understand something, feel free to email me at info@thetwisteddoors.com.

One word of caution for Chapitres 13 and on:

Keep all your lights on!

K.D.

ENTREZ...

Je vois cette vieille maison tous les jours.
Elle est très grande avec un air mystérieux.
En fait, j'ai peur d'elle.

I see this old house every day.
It is very big with a mysterious air.
In fact, I am afraid of it.

je = I
cette maison = this house
elle = she or it (feminine)
elle est = she is; it is
* être = to be
grande = big (feminine)
un = a; one (masculine)

You had better learn how to conjugate the present tense of
the verb **être**. Something tells me you should do it now!
This is friendly advice from me to you.

être = to be

je suis = I am
tu es = you are
il est = he is; it is
elle est = she is; it is
nous sommes = we are
vous êtes = you are
ils sont = they are (masculine)
elles sont = they are (feminine)

Ah! You noticed that there are two ways
to say **you** in French! Let's make this simple:
You use **tu** if you are talking to a friend or to a
family member (that's why it's called **famil**iar).
It is always singular.
You use **vous** (*singular* form) if you are
talking to your teacher, doctor, or a stranger.
It is a sign of respect and politeness.
You also use **vous** (*plural* form) if you
are talking to more than one person,
whether they are familiar or not.

Now, if you haven't learned the **to be** verb, don't
go on! Heed my warning and then take this test!

1. je = _____
2. être = _____
3. vous = _____
4. ils sont = _____
5. maison = _____
6. un = _____
7. tu = _____
8. he is = _____
9. she is = _____
10. I am = _____
11. we are = _____
12. they are = _____
13. you (plural or polite form) are = _____

Here are the answers:

1. I
2. to be
3. you (plural or polite form)
4. they are
5. house
6. one; a
7. you (singular and familiar form)
8. il est
9. elle est
10. je suis
11. nous sommes
12. ils sont or elles sont
13. vous êtes

If you scored 10 out of 13, you are probably
going to be all right. If not, study and retake the test.
You'll see why later! Go to Chapitre 2 if you fared well!

*One asterisk indicates that the word or phrase is not in the French text.
Two asterisks mean that there is an important footnote.
But beware! You must learn it all!*

Je suis anxieuse.
Je décide d'être une fille courageuse.
J'avance vers la grande maison mystérieuse.
J'ai très peur.

I am anxious.
I decide to be a courageous girl.
I walk toward the big mysterious house.
I am very afraid.

je suis = I am
être = to be
une fille = a girl
la = the (before a singular feminine noun)
j'ai = I have
* avoir = to have
très = very
peur = fear
j'ai peur = I am afraid (think: I have fear)

Watch out! For your own good, learn to conjugate the
present tense of the verb **avoir**! Make sure you also learn
the subject pronouns, **je** or **j'** (in front of a vowel or mute **h**),
tu, **il**, **elle**, **nous**, **vous**, **ils**, and **elles**, or you will regret it!

avoir = to have

j'ai = I have
tu as = you have
il a = he has; it has
elle a = she has; it has
nous avons = we have
vous avez = you have
ils ont = they have (masculine)
elles ont = they have (feminine)

Try out this little test. Learn from it now!
It will all come in handy later!
Believe me!

1. fear = _____
2. très = _____
3. la = _____
4. vous avez = _____
5. une fille = _____
6. ils ont = _____
7. ils sont = _____
8. je suis = _____
9. j'ai = _____
10. you (singular, familiar) are = _____
11. you (plural) are = _____
12. il a = _____
13. nous avons = _____
14. tu as = _____
15. I have = _____
16. she has = _____
17. we have = _____
18. they have = _____

Now here are the answers:

1. peur
2. very
3. the
4. you have
5. a girl
6. they have
7. they are
8. I am
9. I have
10. tu es
11. vous êtes
12. he has
13. we have
14. you have
15. j'ai
16. elle a
17. nous avons
18. ils ont or elles ont

If you missed more than 3, go back and take the test again.
When you have succeeded, you may proceed with
caution to Chapitre 3, if you dare!

J'arrive à la grande porte.
Je frappe à la porte deux fois. . .
Un grand homme arrive à la grande porte.
Il ouvre la porte, lentement.
Je vois cet homme.
Il est grand et très vieux.
Il a de petits yeux noirs et un air méchant.

I arrive at the big door.
I knock at the door two times . . .
A tall man arrives at the big door.
He opens the door slowly.
I see this man.
He is tall and very old.
He has little black eyes and a wicked look.

j'arrive = I arrive; I am coming
je frappe = I knock
à = at; to
la porte = the door
deux = two
grand = tall; big (masculine)
un homme = a man
je vois = I see
petit = little (masculine)
noir = black (masculine)

You'd better learn your numbers if you know what is good for you! Friendly advice from me to you! It will pay off later!

un = one
deux = two
trois = three
quatre = four
cinq = five
six = six
sept = seven
huit = eight
neuf = nine
dix = ten

Time is running out! So take this test.
If you missed more than 3,
study and take the test again –
or you will regret it!

1. je vois = _____
2. petit = _____
3. a man = _____
4. la porte = _____
5. je frappe = _____
6. black = _____
7. I am coming = _____
8. little = _____
9. un homme = _____
10. noir = _____
11. j'arrive = _____
12. the door = _____
13. à = _____
14. to = _____
15. deux = _____
16. dix = _____
17. trois = _____
18. cinq = _____
19. quatre = _____
20. sept = _____
21. neuf = _____
22. six = _____

Here are the answers:

1. I see
2. little
3. un homme
4. the door
5. I knock
6. noir
7. j'arrive
8. petit
9. a man
10. black
11. I am coming; I arrive
12. la porte
13. to
14. à
15. two
16. ten
17. three
18. five
19. four
20. seven
21. nine
22. six

If you fared well on the test,
go on to Chapitre 4!

NOTES

« Que voulez-vous?! » dit cet homme avec un air méchant.
« Je suis une petite fille curieuse », dis-je avec une voix tremblante.
« Voulez-vous voir ma maison? Comptez mes doigts, alors! »
J'ai peur mais je compte: vous avez un doigt. Vous avez deux doigts.

Vous avez_____doigts.
Vous avez_____doigts.
Vous avez_____doigts.
Vous avez_____doigts.
Vous avez_____doigts.
Vous avez_____doigts.
Vous avez_____doigts.
Vous avez_____doigts.

« What do you want?! » says this man with a wicked air.
« I am a curious little girl, » I say with a trembling voice.
« Do you want to see my house? Count my fingers, then! »
I am afraid but I count: You have one finger. You have two fingers.

You have three fingers.
You have four fingers.
You have five fingers.
You have six fingers.
You have seven fingers.
You have eight fingers.
You have nine fingers.
You have ten fingers.

Can you finish counting the wicked man's
fingers? If not, you're not allowed to find out if the
little girl enters his house! Warning! You may go
to Chapitre 5 only if you have succeeded!

« Bon, vous comptez mes dix doigts! » dit-il avec une voix méchante.
« Vous êtes une fille curieuse.
Voulez-vous voir ma maison? »
La porte s'ouvre lentement.
Je tremble.

« Good, you are counting my ten fingers! » he says with a mean voice.
« You are a curious girl.
Do you want to see my house? »
The door opens slowly.
I tremble.

vous comptez = you count; you are counting
* compter = to count
il dit = he says
avec = with
une = a; one (feminine)
une **voi**x = a **voi**ce
voulez-vous? = do you want?
voir = to see
lentement = slowly

You had better learn your first **-er** verb, **compter**.
This just means that the verb ends in the letters **er**!
It's not too difficult. Just take the root of the verb, in
this case, **compt**, and add the appropriate ending.
These endings are the same for all regular **-er**
verbs. These endings are shown in **bold** print.

compt**er**** = to count

je compt**e** = I count; I am counting; I do count
tu compt**es** = you count; you are counting; you do count
il compt**e** = he counts; he is counting; he does count
elle compt**e** = she counts; she is counting; she does count
nous compt**ons** = we count; we are counting; we do count
vous compt**ez** = you count; you are counting; you do count
ils compt**ent** = they count; they are counting; they do count
elles compt**ent** = they count; they are counting; they do count

So, the endings for **-er** verbs are
-e, -es, -e, -ons, -ez, -ent.
Notice that **il** and **elle** have the *same* ending.
In this case, they both end with an **e**.
Ils and **elles** also share the same
ending, in this case, **ent**.
Memorize this now if you know what is good for you!

◈

Now take this test! Doing
well on it will be important later on,
if you know what I mean!

1. avec = _____
2. il compte = _____
3. lentement = _____
4. we count = _____
5. une voix = _____
6. voir = _____
7. I count = _____
8. il dit = _____
9. une = _____
10. il compte = _____
11. tu comptes = _____
12. he counts = _____
13. they count (masculine) = _____
14. you (singular, polite) count = _____
15. je compte = _____
16. you (singular, familiar) count = _____

Here are the answers:

1. with
2. he counts
3. slowly
4. nous comptons
5. a voice
6. to see
7. je compte
8. he says
9. a; one
10. he counts
11. you count
12. il compte
13. ils comptent
14. vous comptez
15. I count
16. tu comptes

If you missed more than 3, then practice
and take the test over. Otherwise, go on
to Chapitre 6 to find out what happens
when the little girl enters the house!

** The verbs you have encountered so far all belong to the present tense or more
exactly the *present indicative tense*. This tense simply *indicates* that the action
is occurring at the *present time*. But beware of this tense's translation trap:
Je compte can mean not only **I count**, but also **I am counting** and **I do count**!

La maison est très laide.
Je vois beaucoup de portes en bois.
« Comment vous appelez-vous, ma petite? »
« Je m'appelle Françoise », dis-je avec une voix tremblante.
« Vous êtes dans **ma** maison », dit le vieux monsieur.
« Vous allez rester dans ma grande maison pour toujours! »

The house is very ugly.
I see many wooden doors.
« What is your name, my little one? »
« My name is Françoise, » I say with a trembling voice.
*« You are in **my** house, » says the old gentleman.*
« You are going to stay in my big house forever! »

laide = ugly (feminine)
* laid = ugly (masculine)
beaucoup de = many; a lot of
en = in; made of
le bois = the wood
le = the (before a singular masculine noun)

It's always a good idea to learn how to say, **My name is ____**.
So do it now, if you know what is good for you! This is another
-er verb, so it has the same endings that you have already seen in
Chapitre 5 (compt**er**). One little note: The verb **appeler** means
to call while the verb **s'appeler** means **to call oneself**.

s'appel**er**** = to be named *or* to call oneself

je m'appell**e** = my name is *or* I call myself
tu t'appell**es** = your name is *or* you call yourself
il s'appell**e** = his name is *or* he calls himself
elle s'appell**e** = her name is *or* she calls herself
nous nous appel**ons** = our names are *or* we call ourselves
vous vous appel**ez** = your name(s) is (are) *or* you call yoursel(f)(ves)
ils s'appell**ent** = their names are *or* they call themselves
elles s'appell**ent** = their names are *or* they call themselves

Don't get scared by the single letter **l** in
s'appeler and the double letter **l** in *je m'appelle*.
Just remember that everything takes a double **l** except
the infinitive (*s'appeler)*, the *nous*, and *vous* forms.
What you should be afraid of is not knowing
this chapter! So, take this test!

1. our names are = _____
2. ugly = _____
3. my name is = _____
4. en = _____
5. his name is = _____
6. le = _____
7. bois = _____
8. beaucoup de = _____
9. your (singular, familiar) name is = _____
10. their names are = _____
11. your (plural) names are = _____

Here are the answers:

1. nous nous appelons
2. laid or laide
3. je m'appelle
4. in; made of
5. il s'appelle

16

6. the
7. wood
8. many; a lot of
9. tu t'appelles
10. ils s'appellent or elles s'appellent
11. vous vous appelez

If you missed more than 2, practice and
take the test over. If you did well, you may
proceed with caution to Chapitre 7!

** *S'appeler* is called a reflexive verb (a type of pronominal verb) because the
action of the verb reflects back to the subject such as in **I call myself** or **he
washes himself**. Notice that the subject and the object of the verb are actually
the same person. Pronominal verbs are always conjugated with a reflexive
pronoun. The reflexive pronouns are **me**, **te**, **se**, **nous**, **vous**, and **se**. **Me**
means myself. **Te** means yourself. **Se** can mean himself, herself, oneself, itself,
or themselves. **Nous** means ourselves. **Vous** means yourself or yourselves.
Me, **te**, and **se** become **m'**, **t'**, and **s'** before a vowel or mute **h**.

NOTES

CHAPITRE SEPT 7

La grande porte se ferme derrière moi avec un grand bruit.
Je tire très fort mais elle ne bouge pas!
« Monsieur, laissez-moi sortir de la maison! »
« Mais non, ma petite Françoise, vous allez
rester dans ma grande maison pour toujours! »

The big door closes itself behind me with a big noise.
I pull very hard but it does not move!
« Sir, let me leave the house! »
« I should think not, my little Françoise, you are going
to stay in my big house forever! »

la = the (before singular feminine nouns)
* le = the (before singular masculine nouns)
* les = the (before all plural nouns)
fermer = to close
derrière = behind
moi = me
un = a (before singular masculine nouns)
* une = a (before singular feminine nouns)
un bruit = a noise
tirer = to pull
bo**uge**r = to move (think: **bu**d**ge**)
laissez-moi = let me
sortir = to leave
de = from; of; some
* du (de + le) = from the; of the; some
* des (de + les) = from the; of the; some
dans = in

Nouns are feminine or masculine and singular or plural.
The articles **the** (**le** and **la**) and **a** (**un** and **une**) must agree with the noun.

le is before a masculine singular noun beginning with a consonant.
Example: **le** bruit = **the** noise

la is before a feminine singular noun beginning with a consonant.
Example: **la** maison = **the** house

l' is before any singular noun beginning with a vowel or mute **h**.
Example: **l'**astuce, **l'**homme = **the** shrewdness, **the** man

les is before all plural nouns whether masculine or feminine.
Example: **les** bruits, **les** maisons = **the** noises, **the** houses

un is before a masculine noun: **un** bruit = **a** noise
une is before a feminine noun: **une** maison = **a** house

Not too scared for two more complications?

de means **of, from,** or **some**
But **de** + **le** (**of the**) contracts to a new word **du**
And **de** + **les** (**of the**) contracts to a new word **des**

du (a contraction of **de** + **le**) bruit = [**of the**] [**from the**] [**some**] noise
de la (no contraction) maison = [**of the**] [**from the**] house
de l'homme (no contraction) = [**of the**] [**from the**] man
des (a contraction of **de** + **les**) bruits = [**of the**] [**from the**] [**some**] noises

Last complication (Whew!)

à means **to** or **at**
But **à** + **le** (**to the**) contracts to a new word **au**
And **à** + **les** (**to the**) contracts to a new word **aux**

au (a contraction of **à** + **le**) bruit = **to the** noise
à la (no contraction) maison = **to the** house
à l'homme (no contraction) = **to the** man
aux (a contraction of **à** + **les**) maisons = **to the** houses

20

Now take this test.

1. a noise = _____
2. the noise = _____
3. of the noise = _____
4. to the noise = _____
5. to the noises = _____
6. of the noises = _____
7. to the house = _____
8. to the houses = _____
9. to the man = _____
10. of the man = _____
11. the houses = _____

Here are the answers:

1. un bruit
2. le bruit
3. du bruit
4. au bruit
5. aux bruits
6. des bruits
7. à la maison
8. aux maisons
9. à l'homme
10. de l'homme
11. les maisons

Now watch out! There might be traps in the house
if you use the wrong le, la, les, du, des, au, or aux!
So study! When you have missed no more than 2,
you may proceed with caution to Chapitre 8!

Je suis seule dans cette grande maison!
J'ai très peur. Je ne peux pas sortir de la maison!
Je crie: « Monsieur, je ne suis qu'une petite fille.
Laissez-moi sortir! »
« Mais non, ma petite! »
Il commence à rire.
Tout à coup, il disparaît devant mes yeux!
Est-ce que c'est un fantôme? Je commence à trembler.

I am alone in this big house!
I am very afraid. I cannot get out of the house!
I scream, « Mister, I am only a little girl.
Let me leave! »
« But of course not, my little one! »
He begins to laugh.
Suddenly, he disappears in front of my eyes!
Is this a ghost? I begin to tremble.

seule = alone (feminine)
* seul = alone (masculine)
je peux = I can
je **ne** peux **pas** = I can**not**
je suis = I am
* je **ne** suis **pas** = I am **not**
laissez-moi = let me
sortir = to leave; to get out
mais = but
non = no
commencer = to begin; to start
à = to; at
rire = to laugh
un fantôme = a ghost; a phantom

Have you noticed that putting **ne** before
the verb and **pas** after the verb means **not**?
Now try this test if you're not a fraidy cat!

1. je peux = _____
2. je suis = _____
3. je **ne** suis **pas** = _____
4. je **ne** peux **pas** = _____
5. I am = _____
6. I am not = _____
7. I can = _____
8. I cannot = _____
9. sortir = _____
10. no = _____
11. but = _____
12. to laugh = _____
13. un fantôme = _____
14. laissez-moi = _____
15. to begin = _____
16. to leave = _____
17. a ghost = _____

Here are the answers:

1. I can
2. I am
3. I am not
4. I cannot
5. je suis
6. je ne suis pas
7. je peux
8. je ne peux pas
9. to leave; to get out
10. non
11. mais
12. rire
13. a ghost; a phantom
14. let me
15. commencer
16. sortir
17. un fantôme

If you missed more than 3, take the test again – or else!
If you did well, go on to Chapitre 9.

Je cours vers une porte en bois.
Je frappe très fort! Rien!
Mais je vois écrit sur la porte: **TO HAVE**
Qu'est-ce que ça veut dire?
Je commence avec une voix forte: **

avoir = to have
j'ai = I have
tu as = you have
il a = he has
elle a = she has

Effectivement, la porte commence à bouger!
Donc, je continue:

nous avons = we have
vous avez = you have
ils ont = they have
elles ont = they have

La porte s'ouvre lentement. . .

I run toward a wooden door.
I knock very hard! Nothing!
But I see written on the door: **TO HAVE**
What does that mean?
I begin with a loud voice:
to have = avoir
I have = j'ai
you have = tu as
he has = il a
she has = elle a
Indeed, the door begins to move!
Therefore, I continue:
we have = nous avons
you have = vous avez
they have = ils ont
they have = elles ont
The door opens slowly . . .

je cours = I run
vers = toward
rien = nothing
je vois = I see
écrit = written
ça = that; it (familiar for **cela**)
avec = with
effectivement = indeed (think: **effective**ly)
bouger = to move
donc = therefore
lentement = slowly

Now take this test and check out
the answers below.

1. I have = _____
2. ils ont = _____
3. vous avez = _____
4. tu as = _____
5. she has = _____
6. he has = _____
7. you (plural) have = _____
8. they have (feminine) = _____
9. we have = _____
10. j'ai = _____
11. nous avons = _____
12. you (singular, familiar) have = _____
13. il a = _____
14. elle a = _____

Here are the answers:

1. j'ai
2. they have
3. you have
4. you have
5. elle a
6. il a
7. vous avez
8. elles ont
9. nous avons
10. I have
11. we have
12. tu as
13. he has
14. she has

❖

Did you miss any?
If you did, study and take the test again.
BUT BEWARE:
The wooden door seems to only open itself
when it is given the correct answers . . . *hmm*. So
when you have scored a perfect, you may cautiously
proceed to Chapitre 10 if you want to find out
what is behind this very strange door!

** An alternative translation of the word *with* (**avec**) in this particular sentence is
de (or **d'**): Je commence **d'**une voix forte.

Ça y est! La porte s'ouvre complètement. . .
J'entends quelque chose derrière la porte. Clac!
J'ai tellement peur. Mon cœur bat très vite!
Qu'est-ce que c'est?
La pièce est sombre. J'avance tout doucement.
Je ne peux pas en croire mes yeux.
C'est un petit garçon avec une sucette collée sur la tête!
« Qu'est-ce que tu fais là? »
« Je suis dans cette vieille maison depuis
deux semaines, et je ne peux pas sortir!
Et en plus, la porte m'a fait tomber et maintenant
j'ai une sucette collée sur la tête! »
Le petit garçon commence à pleurer très fort.

That's it! The door opens (itself) completely . . .
I hear something behind the door. Bang!
I am so afraid. My heart is beating very fast!
What is it?
The room is dark. I move forward very carefully.
I cannot believe my eyes.
It's a little boy with a lollipop stuck on his head!
« What are you doing there? »
« I have been in this old house for
two weeks, and I cannot get out!
And what's more, the door made me fall and now
I have a lollipop stuck on my head! »
The little boy begins to cry very hard.

ça y est! = that's it!
quelque chose = something
tellement = so
un cœur = a heart (think: coronary)
vite = quickly; fast
qu'est-ce que **c'est**? = what **is it**?; what is this?
une pièce = a room
sombre = dark
croire = to believe
c' = the abbreviation of **ce** (a demonstrative pronoun)
c'est = it is; that is
c'est un garçon = it is a boy
sur = on
une semaine = a week
pleurer = to cry

Try this little test if you dare! You will
surely need to know how to do this later,
if you know what I mean!

1. what is it? = _____
2. ça y est = _____
3. sombre = _____
4. qu'est-ce que c'est? = _____
5. c'est un garçon = _____
6. un cœur = _____
7. it is a boy = _____
8. it is a room = _____
9. pleurer = _____
10. it is a girl = _____
11. sur = _____

Check out the answers to this test below.
If you missed more than one, study and
take the test again or you will be sorry!

1. qu'est-ce que c'est?
2. that's it
3. dark
4. what is it?; what is this?
5. it is a boy
6. a heart
7. c'est un garçon

8. c'est une pièce
9. to cry
10. c'est une fille
11. on

You may proceed to Chapitre 11 if you feel **very**
secure about knowing this chapter. But
beware! I hear the old man laughing
somewhere in the house!

« Calme-toi », dis-je au petit garçon tout en
tirant très fort sur la sucette collée aux cheveux.
« Comment vous appelez-vous? » dit le petit garçon.
« Je m'appelle Françoise. Comment t'appelles-tu? »
« Je m'appelle Henri. Aïe! Ça me fait mal! »
Tout à coup, nous voyons bouger la porte.
Je crie: « Vite, il faut sortir de cette pièce immédiatement! »
Tout en tirant sur la sucette toujours collée aux
cheveux d'Henri, nous courons dans les grands couloirs
de cette vieille maison laide.
Mais c'est trop tard. Le vieux monsieur nous court après!

« Calm down, » I say to the little boy while
pulling very hard on the lollipop stuck to his hair.
« What is your name? » says the little boy.
« My name is Françoise. What is your name? »
« My name is Henri. Ouch! That hurts! »
Suddenly, we see the door move.
I cry out, « Quickly, it is necessary to leave this room immediately! »
While pulling on the lollipop still stuck to
Henri's hair, we run down the big corridors
of this old ugly house.
But it is too late. The old gentleman is running after us!

la sucette = the lollipop
collé = stuck (masculine)
* la **colle** = the glue
les cheveux = (the) hair
aïe! = ouch!
ça **me** fait mal = that hurts (**me**)
tout à coup = suddenly
il faut = it is necessary
cette** = this or that (before a feminine singular noun)
* ce = this or that (before a masculine singular noun
   that begins with a consonant)
* cet = this or that (before a masculine singular noun
   that begins with a vowel or mute **h**)
* ces = these or those (before all nouns that are plural)
nous courons = we run
* courir = to run
dans = in
le couloir = the corridor; the hall(way) (US)
trop = too; too much
tard = late (think: **tard**y)
après = after

Now here is your first **-ir** verb. This is however an irregular **-ir**
verb because its endings are not typical of a regular **-ir** verb!
But these endings will still aid you in learning many other
irregular **-ir** verbs. Compare these endings to the regular
-ir verb, **réussir**, in Chapitre 30!

cour**ir** = to run

je cour**s** = I run; I am running; I do run
tu cour**s** = you run; you are running; you do run
il, elle cour**t** = he, she, it runs; he is running; he does run
nous cour**ons** = we run; we are running; we do run
vous cour**ez** = you run; you are running; you do run
ils, elles cour**ent** = they run; they are running; they do run

So the endings for some irregular **-ir** verbs are
-s, -s, -t, -ons, -ez, -ent.
Got it?

** *Ce, cet, cette,* and *ces* are demonstrative adjectives.

Now take this test and check your answers below.

1. il faut = _____
2. the hair = _____
3. le couloir = _____
4. nous courons = _____
5. I am running (I run) = _____
6. tu cours = _____
7. you (plural) are running (you run) = _____
8. je cours = _____
9. they are running (they run) (masculine) = _____
10. we are running (we run) = _____
11. I am running (I run) = _____
12. you (singular, familiar) are running (you run) = _____
13. he is running (he runs) = _____
14. vous courez = _____
15. il court = _____
16. this house = _____
17. this man = _____
18. this ghost = _____
19. these houses = _____

Here are the answers. If you missed more
than two, study and take the test again.

1. it is necessary
2. les cheveux
3. the corridor; the hall(way)
4. we are running; we run
5. je cours
6. you are running; you run
7. vous courez
8. I am running; I run
9. ils courent
10. nous courons
11. je cours
12. tu cours
13. il court
14. you are running; you run
15. he runs; he is running
16. cette maison
17. cet homme
18. ce fantôme
19. ces maisons

Did you do well? If so, you may go on to
Chapitre 12. But watch out! The old man is
running after Françoise and Henri in the halls!

NOTES

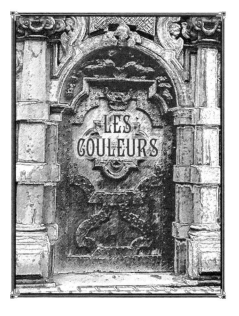

« Ah, vous êtes là mes enfants! »

« Vite, Henri, je vois une porte en bois! »

Mais sur cette porte nous voyons écrit:

LES COULEURS

« Je ne connais pas les couleurs! »

« Moi non plus. »

Mais puisque le vieux monsieur est juste derrière nous,

nous poussons très fort cette porte en bois.

Ça y est. La porte s'ouvre!

Mais qu'est-ce que nous voyons derrière cette porte?

Un grand trou noir!

Qu'est-ce que c'est que ce trou?

Nous allons découvrir. . .

Tout à coup, nous nous trouvons en train de

tomber dans ce grand trou noir.

« Ahhhhh! »

En tombant, nous entendons une voix diabolique:

**« Si vous ouvrez en poussant une porte en bois
qui exige les couleurs,
Ce seront sûrement vos dernières heures! »**

« Ah, you are there my children! »
« Quick, Henri, I see a wooden door! »
But on this door we see written:
THE COLORS
« I don't know the colors! »
« Me neither. »
But since the old gentleman is just behind us,
we push on this wooden door very hard.
That's it. The door opens!
But what do we see behind this door?
A big black hole!
What is this hole?
We are going to find out . . .
Suddenly, we find ourselves (in the process of)
falling in this big black hole.
« Ahhhhh! »
While falling, we hear a diabolical voice:

« If you push open a wooden door that demands the colors, These will surely be your last hours! »

enfants = children
* un enfant = a child (little boy)
* une enfant = a child (little girl)
nous voyons = we see
* voir = to see
moi non plus = me neither
puisque = since
un trou = a hole
nous allons = we go; we are going
en train de = in the process of; busy doing
tomber = to fall
si = if
dernière = last (feminine)

Do you dare try another irregular verb, **voir**?
This verb is classified as an **-oir** verb, not an **-ir** verb!
But notice that the endings of this particular **-oir** verb are
similar to what you have seen in some irregular **-ir** verbs:
-s, -s, -t, -ons, -ez, -ent
Now if you don't want big problems later on,
learn to conjugate this irregular **-oir** verb.

35

v**oir** = to see

je voi**s** = I see; I am seeing; I do see
tu voi**s** = you see; you are seeing; you do see
il, elle voi**t** = he, she, it sees; he is seeing; he does see
nous voy**ons** = we see; we are seeing; we do see
vous voy**ez** = you see; you are seeing; you do see
ils, elles voi**ent** = they see; they are seeing; they do see

Now if you want to find out what happens to
Françoise and Henri after this huge fall, take this test.

1. we see = _____
2. you (singular, familiar) see = _____
3. a child (little boy) = _____
4. moi non plus = _____
5. to fall = _____ _____
6. en train de = _____
7. il voit = _____
8. they see (feminine) = _____
9. vous voyez = _____
10. I see = _____

Here are the answers. If you missed more
than one, study and take the test again
or you will pay!

1. nous voyons
2. tu vois
3. un enfant
4. me neither
5. tomber
6. in the process of
7. he sees
8. elles voient
9. you see
10. je vois

Very uncertain circumstances now await Françoise and Henri
because they forced open a wooden door without correctly
reciting **LES COULEURS**. Dare you proceed to Chapitre 13
to learn about the consequences of their terrible lapse?

NOTES

Je crie: « Aïe! »
« Aïe! » dit Henri.
« Je me suis fait mal aux fesses. »
« Moi aussi. »
« Où sommes-nous? » dit Henri.
Nous regardons bien la pièce.
Elle est totalement vide sauf pour une peinture à l'huile accrochée au mur.
« Henri, cette peinture est très bizarre, regarde-la bien. »

I shout, « Ouch! »
« Ouch! » says Henri.
« I hurt myself on my derriere. »
« Me too. »
« Where are we? » says Henri.
We take a good look at the room.
It is totally empty except for an oil painting hung on the wall.
« Henri, this painting is very bizarre, look at it well. »

je me suis fait mal = I hurt myself
moi aussi = me too
où sommes-nous? = where are we?
regarder = to look at
vide = empty
sauf = except
une peinture = a painting
un mur = a wall

Now, do you remember the endings to an
-er verb? You should! Here are the endings:
-e, **-es**, **-e**, **-ons**, **-ez**, **-ent**
Say this aloud!

Now see if you can figure out for yourself
how to conjugate the following verb:

regard**er** = to look at

je _____
tu _____
il, elle _____
nous _____
vous _____
ils, elles _____

Here is the correct conjugation.

je regard**e** = I look at; I am looking at; I do look at
tu regard**es** = you look at; you are looking at; you do look at
il, elle regard**e** = he, she, it looks at; he is looking at; he does look at
nous regard**ons** = we look at; we are looking at; we do look at
vous regard**ez** = you look at; you are looking at; you do look at
ils, elles regard**ent** = they look at; they are looking at; they do look at

If you want to see what is so bizarre about
the painting on the wall, you may go on
to Chapitre 14. But make sure you know
how to conjugate **-er** verbs first or else!

Nous regardons bien la peinture à l'huile.
Nous voyons quelque chose de très bizarre.
En effet, la peinture semble **vivante**!
Dans la peinture nous voyons un petit garçon habillé en
rouge et bleu en train d'essayer d'ouvrir des portes en bois.
Mais ces portes ne sont pas ordinaires.
Elles sont ***tordues***!
Pourtant, ce n'est pas la seule chose qui est bizarre:
le petit garçon de la peinture ressemble beaucoup à Henri!

We look at the oil painting well.
We see something very bizarre.
*Indeed, the painting seems **alive**!*
In the painting we see a little boy dressed in
red and blue in the process of trying to open wooden doors.
But these doors are not ordinary.
*They are **twisted**!*
However, that is not the only thing that is bizarre:
the little boy in the painting looks very much like Henri!

bien = well
quelque chose = something
en effet = indeed
en train de = in the process of
* être en train de = to be in the process of
* je suis en train de = I am in the process of
ouvrir = to open
tordu = twisted (masculine singular)
ce n'est pas = that is not
la seule chose = the only thing

In the mood to learn your colors?
Remember what happened to Françoise and Henri
when they didn't know their colors? They fell
into a huge hole! So, here is your chance.
Take advantage of it.

rouge = red
jaune = yellow
bleu = blue
orange = orange
blanc = white
noir = black
vert = green

This time you are not going to go on to
the next chapter without a test! So, take
this test if you want to find out about
the very strange live painting!

1. blanc = _____
2. that is = _____
3. that is not = _____
4. to open = _____
5. yellow = _____
6. noir = _____
7. green = _____
8. blue = _____
9. orange = _____
10. we look at = _____
11. I am in the process of . . . = _____

Here are the answers:

1. white
2. c'est
3. ce n'est pas
4. ouvrir
5. jaune
6. black
7. vert
8. bleu
9. orange
10. nous regardons
11. je suis en train de. . .

If you missed no more than 2,
you may proceed to Chapitre 15 to
find out more about this live painting!

« Henri, comment se fait-il que ce tableau soit vivant?
En plus, comment se fait-il que ce soit **toi** là-dedans?
Tu me dis que tu es dans cette maison depuis
deux semaines. Est-ce que tu es sûr de cela? »
Le visage d'Henri devient tout blanc. Les larmes
coulent silencieusement le long de ses petites
joues mignonnes. Mais surtout, les yeux d'Henri
sont remplis d'horreur.

*« Henri, how is it that this painting is alive?
What's more, how come it is **you** inside it?
You tell me that you have been in this house for
two weeks. Are you sure of that? »
Henri's face becomes all white. Tears
run silently along his little
cute cheeks. But especially, Henri's eyes
are filled with horror.*

comment se fait-il que? = how is it that?; how come?
ce soit toi = it is you (subjunctive tense)
* c'est toi = it is you
* c'est moi = it is me
* c'est = it is; that is
là = there
de**dans** = **in**side
là-dedans = inside **there**; in(side) it
depuis = since; for
est-ce que? = is it that?
cela = that; it
le visage = the face
devient = becomes
* devenir = to become
les larmes = the tears
couler = to flow; to run
le long de = along
la joue = the cheek
remplir = to fill

If you put **est-ce que** in front of any statement,
it will turn that statement into a question. Example:

Je suis un garçon. = I am a boy.
Est-ce que je suis un garçon**?** = Am I a boy**?**

If you want to learn the incredible mystery that is
to follow, you had better do well on this test or else!

1. tu es sûr = _____
2. est-ce que tu es sûr? = _____
3. c'est un visage = _____
4. est-ce que c'est un visage? = _____
5. depuis = _____
6. it is you (singular, familiar) = _____
7. c'est moi = _____
8. inside = _____
9. to fill = _____
10. couler = _____
11. les larmes = _____
12. devenir = _____

Here are the answers:

1. you are sure
2. are you sure?
3. it is a face
4. is it a face?
5. since; for
6. c'est toi
7. it is me (I)
8. dedans
9. remplir
10. to flow; to run
11. the tears
12. to become

⊠

This house does not leave room for errors!
If you missed more than 2, go back and try again.
Better to learn it now than later, if you get my drift!
If you are truly ready, you may proceed to Chapitre 16.

« Les portes tordues. . . les portes tordues », répète-t-il.
« Ça me dit quelque chose, vous savez, Françoise. . . »
« Essaie de t'en souvenir, Henri. »
Tout à coup, le vieux monsieur laid ouvre la
porte de cette pièce vide.
*« **Ah! Je vous ai trouvés, mes enfants!** »* rit-il.
Comment pouvons-nous sortir de cette pièce?
Le méchant homme bloque la sortie!
Henri commence à paniquer.
Que devons-nous faire?
Nous ne pouvons pas nous échapper de la pièce!
Je réfléchis: la peinture est vivante. . .
Comment pouvons-nous y entrer pour nous échapper
de cette pièce?
*« Henri! Touchons le tableau vivant! C'est notre
dernier espoir! Vite! »*
Nous le touchons tous les deux ensemble. . .

« The twisted doors . . . the twisted doors, » *he repeats.*
« That reminds me of something, you know, Françoise . . . »
« Try to remember, Henri. »
*Suddenly, the old ugly gentleman opens the
door of this empty room.*
*« **Ah! I have found you, my children!** » he laughs.*
How can we get out of this room?
The wicked man is blocking the exit!
Henri starts to panic.
What must we do?
We can't escape from the room!
I think: the painting is living . . .
*How can we get inside it in order to escape
from this room?*
*« Henri! Let's touch the living painting! It is our
last hope! Quick! »*
We both touch it together . . .

ça me dit quelque chose = that rings a bell; that reminds me of something
vous savez = you know
essayer de = to try to
se souvenir = to remember
pouvons-nous? = can we?
méchant = wicked (masculine)
bloquer = to block (up)
la sortie = the exit
s'échapper de = to escape from
espoir = hope
vite = quickly; quick
tous les deux = both
ensemble = together

Here is the **to remember** verb, **se souvenir**.
Notice that the letter **i** is inserted in all the forms
except for the **nous** and **vous** forms and that the **n**
doubles in the **ils** form. It is another irregular **-ir**
verb with the endings **-s**, **-s**, **-t**, **-ons**, **-ez**, **-ent**.
To see a regular **-ir** verb, go to Chapitre 30!

se souven**ir**** = to remember (to oneself)

je me souvien**s** = I remember (to myself)
tu te souvien**s** = you remember (to yourself)
il, elle se souvien**t** = he, she, it remembers (to himself, herself, itself)
nous nous souven**ons** = we remember (to ourselves)
vous vous souven**ez** = you remember (to yourself or yourselves)
ils, elles se souvien**nent** = they remember (to themselves)

Now take this test.
Check your memory to see if you remember!

1. you (singular, familiar) remember = _____
2. she remembers = _____
3. wicked = _____
4. the exit = _____
5. I remember = _____
6. vite = _____
7. we remember = _____
8. you (singular, polite) remember = _____
9. he remembers = _____
10. ça me dit quelque chose = _____
11. s'échapper de = _____
12. together = _____
13. tous les deux = _____

46

Voici les réponses. (Here are the answers.)

1. tu te souviens
2. elle se souvient
3. méchant
4. la sortie
5. je me souviens
6. quickly
7. nous nous souvenons
8. vous vous souvenez
9. il se souvient
10. that rings a bell; that reminds me of something
11. to escape from
12. ensemble
13. both

Do you want to see what happens when Françoise and Henri touch the painting? Then make sure you do not miss more than 2. If you did, go back, study, and take the test again. Then, when you are ready, you may go on to Chapitre 17 to find out the very strange result that awaits them.

** *Se souvenir* is called an idiomatic pronominal verb. Like all pronominal verbs, it must be conjugated with one of the reflexive pronouns you learned in Chapitre 6: me, te, se, nous, vous, or se.

« Mon Dieu, où sommes-nous? » nous disons tous les deux ensemble.
« C'est tout noir. Je ne vois rien. »
« Moi non plus. »
Nos yeux s'habituent progressivement.
« Attends, Henri. . . Qu'est-ce que c'est? Qu'est-ce que je vois là-bas? »
« C'est une porte, Françoise. »
Je m'approche de la porte.
« Tu as raison, Henri. Regarde cette porte. . . Elle est étrange.
LA PORTE EST TORDUE! »
« Françoise, les portes tordues! Nous avons vu les portes tordues
dans la peinture. . . Ça veut dire que nous sommes
dans le tableau vivant! »
« C'est-à-dire qu'en touchant la peinture,
nous avons réussi à y entrer! »
Nous nous regardons. Le pauvre Henri commence à pleurer.
« Comment pouvons-nous être **dans** un tableau?
C'est impossible! » pleurniche le petit Henri.
Et pourtant, je sais que c'est la seule explication.
« Comment est-ce que nous pouvons en sortir!? » crie Henri.
Mais je n'ai pas beaucoup de temps pour y réfléchir, car
soudain, nous entendons un bruit de grincement terrible:
la porte tordue commence à s'ouvrir toute seule!

« My goodness, where are we? » we both say together.
« It is all black. I don't see anything. »
« Me neither. »
Our eyes progressively get used (to the dark).
« Wait, Henri . . . What is this? What do I see over there? »
« It is a door, Françoise. »
I approach the door.
« You are right, Henri. Look at this door . . . It is strange.
THE DOOR IS TWISTED! »
« Françoise, the twisted doors! We saw the twisted doors
in the painting . . . That means that we are
in the living painting! »
« That is to say that in touching the painting,
we succeeded in entering it! »
We look at each other. Poor Henri begins to cry.
*« How can we be **in** a painting?*
That's impossible! » whimpers little Henri.
And yet, I know that this is the only explanation.
« How can we get out of it!? » Henri cries.
But I do not have much time to think it over, because
suddenly, we hear a terrible creaking noise:
the twisted door begins to open all by itself!

tous = all (masculine plural)
tout = all (masculine singular)
* je **ne** vois **pas** = I do **not** see
je **ne** vois **rien** = I do **not** see **anything**
qu'est-ce que c'est? = what is this?
là-bas = over there
tu **as** raison = you are right (think: you **have** reason)
ça veut dire = that means; it means
c'est-à-dire = that is to say
pleurer = to cry
pourtant = yet; nevertheless
beaucoup = a lot; (very) much
le temps = (the) time
beaucoup de temps = a lot of time; much time
réfléchir = to think; to **reflec**t
tout**e** seul**e** = all alone (**feminine**)
* tout seul = all alone (masculine)

If you know what is good for you, you had
better learn how to say **to be right**. Watch out!
In French you say **I have reason**, not I **am** right.

avoir raison = to be right

j'**ai** raison = I am right
tu **as** raison = you are right
il, elle **a** raison = he, she is right
nous **avons** raison = we are right
vous **avez** raison = you are right
ils, elles **ont** raison = they are right

Now take this test. Study well first!

1. là-bas = _____
2. il a raison = _____
3. pleurer = _____
4. qu'est-ce que c'est? = _____
5. he is right = _____
6. I am right = _____
7. beaucoup = _____
8. le temps = _____
9. we are right = _____
10. ça veut dire = _____
11. réfléchir = _____
12. je ne vois pas = _____

Voici les réponses. (Here are the answers.)

1. over there
2. he is right
3. to cry
4. what is this?
5. il a raison
6. j'ai raison
7. a lot; much
8. (the) time
9. nous avons raison
10. that means; it means
11. to think
12. I do not see

If you missed more than 2, go back and study
hard! Then take the test again. When you are ready,
you may go on to Chapitre 18 to find out about
the opening, creaking, twisted door!

NOTES

Henri se lance contre moi. Je perçois les tremblements
de son malheureux petit corps.
J'essaie moi-même d'être courageuse, mais franchement,
je suis effrayée.
La porte tordue continue son grincement atroce. . .
J'ai envie de me couvrir les oreilles.
Malgré cette terreur, nous avançons vers la porte.
Tout à coup, j'entends un cri d'Henri:
« Françoise, regardez! C'est dehors! »
La porte tordue étant complètement ouverte,
nous pouvons apercevoir le ciel.
Nous avançons encore deux ou trois pas.
Nous sommes dehors.
« Regardez le ciel, Françoise. . . C'est tout violet.
Et les nuages, ils sont énormes et jaunes.
Et le vent, ça souffle fort dans mes oreilles.
Et le. . . »
« Arrête à la fin, Henri! Écoute bien! » je chuchote.
« On dirait que le vent siffle *ton nom!* »
En effet nous entendons: « H e n r i . . . H e n r i . . . H e n r i . . . »

Henri throws himself against me. I perceive the trembling
of his poor (unhappy) little body.
I (myself) try to be courageous, but frankly,
I am frightened.
The twisted door continues its atrocious creaking . . .
I feel like covering my ears.
Despite this terror, we walk toward the door.
All of a sudden, I hear a cry from Henri:
« Françoise, look! It is the outside! »
The twisted door being completely open,
we can perceive the sky.

We advance again two or three steps.
We are outside.
« Look at the sky, Françoise . . . It is all purple.
And the clouds, they are enormous and yellow.
And the wind, it's blowing hard in my ears.
And the . . . »
« Stop already, Henri! Listen carefully! » I whisper.
« One would say that the wind is whistling your name! »
Indeed we hear, « H e n r i . . . H e n r i . . . H e n r i . . . »

lancer = to throw
malheureux = unhappy
moi-même = myself
j'ai envie de = I feel like
* avoir envie de = to feel like
* il a envie de pleurer = he feels like crying
dehors = outside
le ciel = the sky
un pas = a step; a pace
un nuage = a cloud
le vent = the wind (think: **vent**ilation)
souffler = to blow
siffler = to whistle
violet = purple; violet (masculine)
* violett**e** = purple; violet (**feminine**)
jaune = yellow (masculine and feminine)
* rouge = red (masculine and feminine)
* vert**e** = green (**feminine**)
* bleu**e** = blue (**feminine**)
* brun**e** = brown (**feminine**)
* blanch**e** = white (think: blank; bleach) (**feminine**)
* noir**e** = black (**feminine**)
* rose = pink (masculine and feminine)
* orange = orange (masculine and feminine)
* gris**e** = gray (**feminine**)

Now, if I tell you that **j'ai envie de pleurer** means *I feel like crying*,
and **il a envie de pleurer** means *he feels like crying*, then see
if you can figure out how to do the sentences below yourself!
Hint: You have to conjugate the **avoir (to have)** verb first.

1. I feel like crying
2. you (singular, familiar) feel like crying
3. he, she feels like crying
4. we feel like crying
5. you (plural) feel like crying
6. they feel like crying

So, all you do is conjugate the **avoir** verb and
then add **envie de** followed by the verb's infinitive
form which in this example is *to cry* or **pleurer**.
That's it! Study the answers below.

1. j'***ai* envie de** pleurer
2. tu ***as* envie de** pleurer
3. il, elle ***a* envie de** pleurer
4. nous ***avons* envie de** pleurer
5. vous ***avez* envie de** pleurer
6. ils, elles ***ont* envie de** pleurer

Now take this test.

1. nous avons envie de siffler = _____
2. les nuages sont violets = _____
3. the sky is blue = _____
4. la porte est jaune = _____
5. they feel like looking at (masculine) = _____
6. les oreilles sont roses = _____
7. I feel like crying = _____
8. you (singular, familiar) feel like throwing = _____
9. orange = _____
10. brown (masculine) = _____
11. white (masculine) = _____
12. green (feminine) = _____
13. black (masculine) = _____
14. red = _____
15. to blow = _____
16. malheureux = _____
17. myself = _____
18. gray (masculine) = _____

Voici les réponses:

1. we feel like whistling
2. the clouds are purple (or violet)
3. le ciel est bleu
4. the door is yellow

 5. ils ont envie de regarder
 6. the ears are pink
 7. j'ai envie de pleurer
 8. tu as envie de lancer
 9. orange
10. brun
11. blanc
12. verte
13. noir
14. rouge
15. souffler
16. unhappy
17. moi-même
18. gris

Hard enough for you?
You cannot go on if you missed more than three.
If you did, go back and study. Then take the test
again. When you are ready, you may proceed at
your own risk to Chapitre 19 to find out what
Françoise and Henri are going to find!

« Mon Dieu, Henri. Regarde autour de nous.
Nous sommes dans un cimetière! »
Le vent continue à siffler: « Henri. . . Henri. . . »
Il y a des tombeaux partout. Il y a des pierres tombales
de toutes tailles, de toutes sortes.
« Qu'est-ce que c'est que ce cimetière? » dit Henri d'un air soucieux.
« Je ne l'aime pas.
Je veux rentrer à l'intérieur », dit-il comme un enfant gâté.
« Tu veux rentrer? Ne me fais pas rire, Henri.
Où veux-tu rentrer exactement? »
« Je ne sais pas mais. . . »
« Oh, tais-toi. Tu sais bien que. . . »
Je cesse de répondre à Henri car mon œil est tout de suite
attiré par une pierre tombale qui n'est pas comme les autres.
En effet, son épitaphe est assez curieuse
comme en témoigne l'inscription suivante:

Il n'a pas attendu
Que s'ouvre la porte tordue
Tant pis pour lui
Il restera toujours ici

On se regarde. Qu'est-ce que cela veut dire?
Qui n'a pas attendu?

« My goodness, Henri. Look around us.
We are in a cemetery! »
The wind continues to whistle, « Henri . . . Henri . . . »
There are tombs everywhere. There are tombstones
of all sizes, of all sorts.
« What's this cemetery? » says Henri with a worried look.
« I don't like it.
I want to go back inside (the old house), » he says like a spoiled child.
« You want to go back in? Don't make me laugh, Henri.
Where do you want to go back in, exactly? »
« I don't know but . . . »
« Oh, be quiet. You know very well that . . . »
I stop answering Henri because my eye is immediately
attracted to a tombstone that is not like the others.
Indeed, its epitaph is quite curious
as can be witnessed by the following inscription:

He did not wait
For the twisted door to open
Too bad for him
He will stay here forever

We look at each other. What does that mean?
Who *did not wait?*

autour = around
il y a = there is; there are
partout = everywhere
une pierre = a stone
un air = a look
soucieux = worried
rentrer = to re-enter a place; to go (or come) back in
gâté = spoiled (masculine)
faire = to do; to make
un œil = an eye
tout de suite = immediately
attirer = to attract
attendre = to wait (for)
tant pis = too bad

Now you are going to learn the **to do** or **to make** verb, **faire**.
Watch out, because it is tricky. But if you want to find
out what happens in the cemetery, learn it now!

faire = to do; to make

je fai**s** = I do, I am doing; I make, I am making
tu fai**s** = you do, you are doing; you make, you are making
il, elle fai**t** = he, she, it does, he is doing; he, she, it makes, he is making
nous fais**ons** = we do, we are doing; we make, we are making
vous faites = you do, you are doing; you make, you are making
ils, elles font = they do, they are doing; they make, they are making

Did you see how tricky **vous faites** and
ils font are? But to get anywhere in this place,
you had better remember these conjugations!
Now take this test.

 1. immediately = _____
 2. partout = _____ ____ _____
 3. un œil = _____
 4. a look = _____
 5. he makes = _____
 6. I do = _____
 7. you (plural) make = _____
 8. they do (masculine) = _____
 9. you (singular, familiar) make = _____
10. soucieux = _____
11. we do = _____
12. tant pis = _____

Voici les réponses:

 1. tout de suite
 2. everywhere
 3. an eye
 4. un air
 5. il fait
 6. je fais
 7. vous faites
 8. ils font
 9. tu fais
10. worried
11. nous faisons
12. too bad

If you missed more than one, go back and
take the test again. Then, when you are
really ready, you may go on and try to
decipher the epitaph in Chapitre 20!

« **Il n'a pas attendu que s'ouvre la porte tordue** », chuchote Henri.
Je vois que le visage d'Henri devient tout pâle. Sa lèvre inférieure
tremble. Il regarde vers le ciel comme pour obtenir une
réponse logique à toutes ses questions. Il baisse ses yeux bleus
et puis il fixe son regard sur moi.
« C'est moi, Françoise. C'est moi qui n'ai pas attendu que
la porte tordue s'ouvre! Françoise, je crois que je suis
dans cette vieille maison depuis bien plus de deux semaines! »
Je le prends doucement par les épaules.
« Henri, est-ce que tu te souviens de quelque chose?
Dis-moi! »
Henri me regarde encore et il me répond
presque trop calmement:
« Oui, je me souviens de quelque chose. . . »

« *He did not wait for the twisted door to open*, » *whispers Henri.*
I see that Henri's face becomes completely pale. His lower lip
trembles. He looks toward the sky as if to obtain a
logical answer to all his questions. He lowers his blue eyes
and then he fixes his gaze upon me.
« *It is me, Françoise. It is me who did not wait for*
the twisted door to open! Françoise, I think that I have been
in this old house for much more than two weeks! »
I take him gently by the shoulders.
« *Henri, do you remember something?*
Tell me! »
Henri looks at me again and he answers me
almost too calmly:
« *Yes, I remember something . . .* »

chuchoter = to whisper (think: shhh)
le visage = the face
la lèvre = the lip
comme = like; as (if)
baisser = to lower
les yeux = the eyes
puis = then
bien = well
plus = more
bien plus = much more
doucement = gently
les épaules = the shoulders
presque = almost; **near**ly

Now you must learn the other parts of the body if
you want to find out what poor Henri remembers!

la tête = the head
le nez = the nose
la bouche = the mouth
la joue = the cheek
les cheveux = the hair
le bras = the arm
la **ma**in = the hand (think: **man**ufacture)
la jambe = the leg
le **pi**ed = the foot (think: **ped**estrian)
les oreilles = the ears

Study hard to learn all these words.
You won't be sorry later!
Now take this test.

1. les épaules = _____
2. the eyes = _____
3. le visage = _____
4. la tête = _____
5. the lip = _____
6. the foot = _____
7. the hand = _____
8. les cheveux = _____
9. the arm = _____
10. le pied = _____
11. the mouth = _____
12. la jambe = _____
13. the nose = _____
14. the cheek = _____
15. the ears = _____

Voici les résponses:

1. the shoulders
2. les yeux
3. the face
4. the head
5. la lèvre
6. le pied
7. la main
8. the hair
9. le bras
10. the foot
11. la bouche
12. the leg
13. le nez
14. la joue
15. les oreilles

If you missed more than 2, go back and study.
Then take the test again. When you are ready,
you may go on to Chapitre 21.

NOTES

CHAPITRE VINGT ET UN 21

Le ciel devient tout noir autour de nous.
Les volumineux nuages verts traversent le ciel
à une vitesse effroyable. Mais c'est surtout le vent qui
nous fait perdre courage car il siffle très nettement et avec une
force épouvantable: « **HENRI. . . HENRI!** »
« Vite, Henri! Cet orage sinistre va nous tuer!
Tu **dois** te souvenir de quelque chose! »
Sans émotion, sans dire un mot, le petit Henri avance
lentement vers la pierre tombale. Il tend sa petite main
et commence à enlever la poussière qui couvre la
partie inférieure de la pierre.
« Henri, ce n'est vraiment pas le moment de faire le ménage! »
dis-je presque en pleurant.
« Tu m'entends? Henri! Réponds-moi! »
Henri se tourne vers moi un instant.
Il fait deux pas en arrière.
Puis, je la vois! Il y a une autre inscription!

*The sky becomes completely black around us.
The voluminous green clouds cross the sky
at a horrifying speed. But it is especially the wind that
causes us to lose heart because it whistles very clearly and with an
appalling force, « **HENRI . . . HENRI!** »
« Quick, Henri! This sinister storm is going to kill us!
You **must** remember something! »
Without emotion, without saying a word, little Henri advances
slowly toward the tombstone. He holds out his little hand
and starts to remove the dust that covers the
bottom portion of the stone.
« Henri, this is really not the time to do housework! »
I say almost crying.
« Do you hear me? Henri! Answer me! »
Henri turns toward me (for) an instant.
He takes two steps backwards.
Then, I see it! There is another inscription!*

autour = around
les nuages = the clouds
traverser = to cross
la vitesse = the speed
effroyable = horrifying
surtout = especially
qui = who; that; which
perdre **courage** = to lose heart; to become dis**courage**d
le courage = the courage; the bravery
car = because
tuer = to kill
sans = without
la pierre = the stone
la poussière = the dust
couvrir = to cover
le ménage = the housework
se tourner vers = to turn toward
en arrière = backwards
puis = then

Now you are going to learn the expression
il y a. It means **there is** or **there are**.
Here are some examples:

il y a un tombeau dans le cimetière = there is a tomb in the cemetery
il y a des tombeaux partout = there are tombs everywhere
il y a des nuages dans le ciel = there are clouds in the sky
il y a une pierre par terre = there is a stone on the ground

Get it? Now take this test!

1. there is a door in the house = _____
2. il y a une inscription sur la pierre tombale = _____
3. traverser = _____
4. la vitesse = _____
5. autour = _____
6. surtout = _____
7. backwards = _____
8. without = _____
9. to kill = _____
10. then = _____
11. the stone = _____
12. la poussière = _____

Voici les réponses:

1. il y a une porte dans la maison
2. there is an inscription on the tombstone
3. to cross
4. the speed
5. around
6. especially
7. en arrière
8. sans
9. tuer
10. puis
11. la pierre
12. the dust

If you missed more than 1, go back, study, and take the test again. Otherwise, you cannot go on to Chapitre 22 to find out what this new inscription reveals!

Nous ne faisons attention ni à l'orage redoutable qui s'approche de nous,
ni au vent infernal qui continue à siffler le nom d'Henri. Notre
attention se fixe sur cette pierre tombale grise, morbide, qui
a bien caché son secret sous la poussière depuis
un temps indéterminé:

Ici repose l'esprit d'Henri
Pour le libérer
Appuyez *IcI*

« Ah, je le savais, Françoise! Voici la preuve que je suis
dans cette maison depuis bien plus de deux semaines!
Mon nom est inscrit sur cette pierre tombale! »
Henri frissonne avec terreur.
Comment puis-je le consoler?
Après tout, son nom est bien inscrit sur cette pierre. . .
Qu'est-ce que cela veut dire? Est-ce que mon pauvre
Henri n'est plus de ce monde? Je m'efforce de lui cacher
mes vrais sentiments. Ce serait épouvantable d'être à sa place.
Je retrouve mon courage:
« Ne t'en fais pas, Henri. Nous allons sortir de cette situation.
Tu vas voir! »
Le petit Henri essaie de sourire. . . mais il n'y arrive pas.
Je vois la sueur former de petites gouttes sur son front.
« Françoise, est-ce que c'est trop tard? Est-ce que je suis
déjà mort? Aidez-moi! Je vous en supplie! »
Je n'en peux plus.
Les paroles d'Henri m'envahissent d'émotion.
Je commence à pleurer malgré moi.
Henri se rend compte de ce qu'il m'a fait.

Un peu vexé, il se redresse et avance comme
un petit soldat vers le tombeau.
Je l'entends relire l'inscription à haute voix:

Ici repose l'esprit d'Henri
Pour le libérer
Appuyez *IcI*

« Où faut-il appuyer?! » dit-il, perplexe.
« Tu ne vois pas, Henri? » je lui réponds en pleurnichant.
« C'est évident! »

We pay neither attention to the dreadful storm that approaches us,
nor to the infernal wind that continues to whistle Henri's name. Our
attention focuses upon this gray, morbid tombstone that
has well hidden its secret under the dust for
an undetermined (amount of) time:

Here lies the spirit of Henri
In order to free it
Press *Here*

« Ah, I knew it, Françoise! Here is the proof that I have been
in this house for much more than two weeks!
My name is inscribed on this tombstone! »
Henri shivers with terror.
How can I comfort him?
After all, his name is indeed engraved on this stone . . .
What does this mean? Is my poor
Henri no longer of this world? I force myself to hide from him
my true feelings. It would be dreadful to be in his place.
I regain my courage:
« Don't worry about it, Henri. We are going to get out of this situation.
You're going to see! »
Little Henri tries to smile . . . but he doesn't succeed.
I see sweat form little drops on his forehead.
« Françoise, is it too late? Am I
already dead? Help me! I beg you! »
I can't go on any more.
Henri's words overcome me with emotion.
I begin to cry despite myself.
Henri realizes what he has done to me.

A little hurt, he straightens himself up and advances like
a little soldier toward the tomb.
I hear him re-read the engraving aloud:

Here lies the spirit of Henri
In order to free it
Press *Here*

« *Where do we have to press?!* » *he says perplexed.*
« *Don't you see, Henri?* » *I answer him while sniveling.*
« *It's obvious!* »

ne. . . ni. . . ni = neither . . . nor
un orage = a (thunder)storm
redoutable = dreadful
cacher = to hide
sous = under
voici = here is
la **pr**euve = the **pr**oof
ce monde = this world
re**trouver** = to find again; to regain
* **trouver** = to find
sourire = to smile
la sueur = the sweat
une goutte = a drop
le front = the forehead
déjà = already
supplier = to beg
les paroles = the words
envahir = to invade; to overcome
malgré = despite
vexer = to hurt; to offend

Now you are going to learn two regular **-re** verbs.
Their endings are **-s**, **-s**, no ending, **-ons**, **-ez**, **-ent**.

entend**re** = to hear

j'entend**s** = I hear; I am hearing; I do hear
tu entend**s** = you hear; you are hearing; you do hear
il, elle entend = he, she, it hears; he is hearing; he does hear
nous entend**ons** = we hear; we are hearing; we do hear
vous entend**ez** = you hear; you are hearing; you do hear
ils, elles entend**ent** = they hear; they are hearing; they do hear

répond**re** = to answer

je répond**s** = I answer; I am answering; I do answer
tu répond**s** = you answer; you are answering; you do answer
il, elle répond = he, she, it answers; he is answering; he does answer
nous répond**ons** = we answer; we are answering; we do answer
vous répond**ez** = you answer; you are answering; you do answer
ils, elles répond**ent** = they answer; they are answering; they do answer

Do you see how the endings are the same for both verbs? Now is the time to learn these verbs and memorize their endings. You will see why later!

Study hard and take this test.

1. malgré = _____
2. ce monde = _____
3. the proof = _____
4. the sweat = _____
5. vexer = _____
6. to find again = _____
7. une goutte = _____
8. under = _____
9. redoutable = _____
10. I am hearing = _____
11. ils répondent = _____
12. you (singular, familiar) are hearing = _____
13. he answers = _____
14. nous répondons = _____
15. we hear = _____
16. you (plural) answer = _____

Voici les réponses:

1. despite
2. this world
3. la preuve
4. la sueur
5. to hurt; to offend
6. retrouver
7. a drop
8. sous
9. dreadful

10. j'entends
11. they answer
12. tu entends
13. il répond
14. we answer
15. nous entendons
16. vous répondez

If you missed more than two, you cannot go on to
Chapitre 23 to find out where (and what) they
need to press in order to free Henri's spirit!
You must study and take the test again.
Then when you have passed the test,
you may proceed to Chapitre 23!

NOTES

« *IcI*, Henri! » dis-je en oubliant mon chagrin.

« Regarde bien comme l'inscription du mot *IcI* est penchée
d'une façon curieuse. Du reste, l'épitaphe dit bien d'appuyer *IcI!* »
Contente de moi, je me dépêche d'appuyer
sur ce mot curieusement façonné. . .
Mais cette action est brusquement interrompue
par un coup de vent qui me fait tourner comme une toupie!
Toujours un peu étourdie, je me rends compte que je suis
la seule victime du vent. Henri lui échappe complètement.
Il ne prend même pas conscience de ce qui m'est arrivée.

« Oh! Comme le vent est bizarre!
Si je ne savais pas. . . »

« Attendez, Françoise! » crie Henri.
Il semble voir quelque chose.
Henri se penche pour examiner de plus près l'inscription, *IcI*.
Puis il me regarde d'un air perplexe.

« Vous avez raison, Françoise. Ce mot est gravé d'une façon particulière.
Les lettres *I* semblent former les côtés d'un objet! »
Instinctivement, il pose le bout des doigts sur les lettres.
Je le vois palper ces lettres avec soin.
Soudain, il se lève en criant:

« Françoise, c'est une porte tordue miniature déguisée en lettres! »
**« Henri, alors c'est là qu'il faut appuyer
pour te sauver! »**
Je saute vers la pierre tombale pour
vite appuyer sur ce déguisement surprenant.
Et vlan!
Je vois une lumière éblouissante accompagnée d'une
douleur abdominale qui me coupe le souffle.
C'est le petit Henri qui m'attaque!

« NON! ARRÊTEZ, FRANÇOISE! Souvenez-vous de
l'épitaphe?! Il faut attendre que la porte tordue s'ouvre
d'elle-même! Sinon, vous serez prisonnière comme moi
dans cette maison diabolique pour toujours! »

Enfin. . .
Henri se souvient de pourquoi il est prisonnier:
il a ouvert une porte tordue. C'est tout. Un acte bien innocent.
Et maintenant, il vient de me sauver du même
destin que lui.

« **IcI** (Here), Henri! » I say while forgetting my sorrow.
« Look carefully at how the inscription of the word **IcI** is slanted
in a curious way. What's more, the epitaph does indeed say to press **IcI**! »
Pleased with myself, I hurry to press down
on this curiously fashioned word . . .
But this action is abruptly interrupted
by a gust of wind that causes me to spin around like a top!
Still a little bit dizzy, I realize that I am
the only victim of the wind. Henri completely escapes it.
He doesn't even become aware of what happened to me
« Oh! How the wind is bizarre!
If I didn't know . . . »
« Wait, Françoise! » cries out Henri.
He seems to see something.
Henri leans over so as to more closely examine the inscription, **IcI**.
Then he looks at me with a perplexed air.
« You are right, Françoise. This word is engraved in a peculiar way.
The letters **I** seem to form the sides of an object! »
Instinctively, he places the tip of his fingers on the letters.
I see him palpate these letters with care.
Suddenly, he gets up while shouting,
« Françoise, it's a miniature twisted door disguised as letters! »
**« Henri, then that's where we have to press
in order to save you! »**
I jump toward the tombstone in order to
quickly press down on this amazing disguise.
Wham!
I see a dazzling light accompanied by an
abdominal pain that knocks the breath out of me.
It is little Henri who is attacking me!
« **NO! STOP, FRANÇOISE!** Remember
the epitaph?! You have to wait for the twisted door to open
by itself! If not, you will be a prisoner like me
in this diabolical house forever! »
Finally . . .
Henri remembers why he is (a) prisoner:
he opened a twisted door. That's all. A really innocent act.
And now, he just saved me from the same
destiny as his.

ici = here
oublier = to forget
chagrin = sorrow; grief
penchée = slanted (feminine)
la **façon** = the way
appuyer = to press
se dépêcher = to hurry (up) (oneself)
façonner = to make; to **fa**shi**on**; to manufacture
coup de vent = gust of wind
* un **coup** = a hit; a knock; a blow
se rendre compte = to realize
échapper à = to **escap**e (from)
se **pench**er = to lean over
de **plus près** = closer; **more close**ly
près = close (by); near(by)
le côté = the side
poser = to put (down); to place
se **lev**er = to get up (think: e**lev**ator)
il faut = it is necessary; we have to; we must; you have to; you must
sauv**e**r = to **save**
surprenant = **surpr**ising; amazing
une **lumi**ère = a light (think: il**lumi**nation)
la douleur = the pain
me **coup**er le souffle = to **knock** the breath out of me
souffle = breath
* **souffle**r = to blow
pourquoi = why
même = same; even
le **destin** = (the) **destin**y; the fate

How do you feel about **-er** verbs?
See how well you do now with the verbs below.
If you remember your endings, you
should have no trouble conjugating the
following verbs:

sauver
poser
souffler

After you conjugate these three verbs,
take this test!

1. coup = _____
2. échapper à = _____
3. se rendre compte = _____
4. the pain = _____

5. to fashion or to make = _____

6. gust of wind = _____

7. the light = _____

8. near = _____

9. le côté = _____

10. it is necessary = _____

11. here = _____

Voici les réponses:

sauv**er** = to save
je sauv**e** = I save; I am saving; I do save
tu sauv**es** = you save; you are saving; you do save
il, elle sauv**e** = he, she, it saves; he is saving; he does save
nous sauv**ons** = we save; we are saving; we do save
vous sauv**ez** = you save; you are saving; you do save
ils, elles sauv**ent** = they save; they are saving; they do save

pos**er** = to put (down); to place
je pos**e** = I put; I am putting; I do put
tu pos**es** = you put; you are putting; you do put
il, elle pos**e** = he, she, it puts; he is putting; he does put
nous pos**ons** = we put; we are putting; we do put
vous pos**ez** = you put; you are putting; you do put
ils, elles pos**ent** = they put; they are putting; they do put

souffl**er** = to blow
je souffl**e** = I blow; I am blowing; I do blow
tu souffl**es** = you blow; you are blowing; you do blow
il, elle souffl**e** = he, she, it blows; he is blowing; he does blow
nous souffl**ons** = we blow; we are blowing; we do blow
vous souffl**ez** = you blow; you are blowing; you do blow
ils, elles souffl**ent** = they blow; they are blowing; they do blow

1. hit; knock; blow
2. to escape (from)
3. to realize
4. la douleur
5. façonner
6. coup de vent
7. la lumière
8. près
9. the side
10. il faut
11. ici

You are allowed to miss only one on the
vocabulary words and none on the conjugation
in order to go on to Chapitre 24. So, study and
take the test again if you want to find out
what happens in this eerie cemetery!

Je reprends mon souffle. Je me mets debout.
L'orage est de plus en plus proche. Un éclair peint sa mince
trajectoire contre le ciel bien noir. Le tonnerre suit avec
un éclat qui me fait mal aux oreilles. Le vent fait des tourbillons
de poussière et de débris tout en sifflant: « Henri. . . Henri. . . »
Je sais intuitivement que nous n'avons pas beaucoup de temps.
Il faut sortir de ce cimetière ou mourir.
Cette petite porte tordue est notre seul espoir.
Nous ne pouvons pas l'ouvrir nous-mêmes. Comment la faire ouvrir?
J'avance vers la porte miniature.
J'essaie de l'examiner de très près.
Avons-nous manqué de découvrir la clé de quelque chose?
Henri vient me rejoindre. Il ne sait pas que nous sommes
en danger de mort. C'est bien qu'il ne s'en rende pas compte.
Je le vois réexaminer la petite porte.
« Françoise, je crois avoir trouvé quelque chose d'écrit
sur cette porte. C'est très petit. . . J'arrive à peine à la lire. »
Il épelle lentement et soigneusement chaque lettre:
« ê-t-r-e »
Quelle ironie! Y a-t-il quelqu'un qui se moque de nous?

✦

I get my breath back. I stand up.
The storm is closer and closer. A flash of lightning paints its thin
trajectory against the very dark sky. The thunder follows with
a burst that hurts my ears. The wind makes whirlwinds
of dust and debris while whistling, « Henri . . . Henri . . . »
I know intuitively that we don't have much time.
We have to get out of this cemetery or die.
This little twisted door is our only hope.
We cannot open it ourselves. How do we make it open?
I walk toward the miniature door.
I try to examine it close up.
Have we missed discovering the key (clue) to something?
Henri comes to join me. He doesn't know that we are
in mortal danger. It's good that he doesn't realize this.
I see him re-examine the little door.
« Françoise, I believe that I have found something written
on this door. It is very small . . . I can barely read it. »
He spells out each letter slowly and carefully:
« t-o b-e »
How ironic! Is there someone (who is) mocking us?

✦

se mettre debout = to stand up
* mettre = to put
debout = standing (up)
un orage = a (thunder)storm
proche = close (by)
un éclair = a flash or streak of lightning
mince = thin
contrc = against (think: pros and **con**s)
suivre = to follow
un éclat = a burst
il faut = it is necessary; we have to; we must
sortir = to get out; to leave
ou = or
mour**ir** = to die (think: **mor**tal)
nous-mêmes = **our**selves
manquer = to miss
la **clé** = the key; the **clue**
trouver = to find
à peine = barely; hardly
lire = to read (think: **lit**er**a**cy)
épeler = to spell (out)
soigneusement = carefully
* **soin** = care
y a-t-il? = is there?; are there?
quelqu'**un** = some**one**; somebody

If you know what is good for you,
you must learn to conjugate the verb **sortir**.
It is an irregular **-ir** verb. Do you remember the
endings for many irregular **-ir** verbs?

sort**ir** = to go out; to leave; to get out; to exit; to come out

je sor**s** = I exit; I am exiting; I do exit
tu sor**s** = you exit; you are exiting; you do exit
il, elle sor**t** = he, she, it exits; he is exiting; he does exit
nous sort**ons** = we exit; we are exiting; we do exit
vous sort**ez** = you exit; you are exiting; you do exit
ils, elles sort**ent** = they exit; they are exiting; they do exit

Now take this test.

1. il faut = _____
2. a thunderstorm = _____
3. the key = _____
4. un éclat = _____
5. to get out = _____
6. it is necessary to miss = _____
7. it is necessary to find = _____
8. il faut sortir = _____
9. to read = _____
10. care = _____
11. against = _____
12. quelqu'un = _____

Voici les réponses:

1. it is necessary
2. un orage
3. la clé
4. a burst
5. sortir
6. il faut manquer
7. il faut trouver
8. it is necessary to leave
9. lire
10. soin
11. contre
12. someone; somebody

You are only allowed to miss
one in order to go on to Chapitre 25.
So, study and take the test again if you
want to discover who might be mocking
Françoise and Henri in the cemetery!

Être. . . Une référence shakespearienne qui se moque de nous.
Heureusement, Henri est trop petit pour comprendre. . .
Le vent incessant qui souffle en tempête me rappelle ma mortalité.
Je dois agir vite. Je vais donner à la petite porte tordue
ce qu'elle veut pour nous sauver. Je m'agenouille devant la
porte miniature et je déclare:

« être = to be
je suis = I. . . »

Soudain, il y a une rafale de vent si intense que c'est
intolérable. Je me couvre la figure avec les mains
pour me protéger et puis j'entends la voix monstrueuse du vent:

« **HENRI. . . HENRI. . . HENRI!** »

Je réfléchis un instant et **enfin** je comprends!
« C'est ça!
Henri, le vent siffle ton nom pour te dire que
*c'est à **toi** de faire ouvrir cette porte tordue!*
Pas moi!
Ton **existence**, ton bien-**être** sont en jeu! »
Henri a l'air de comprendre. À son tour,
il s'agenouille devant la porte tordue. . .
Tout à coup, il commence à faire très froid.
Nous ressentons une vibration tout autour de nous.
« Françoise, **qu'est-ce que c'est?** »
Puis nous entendons une voix démoniaque qui résonne
comme le tonnerre:

« Ah, mon petit Henri! Françoise a tort!
Si vous l'écoutez, vous mourrez tous les deux! »

To be . . . *A Shakespearean reference that laughs at us.*
Fortunately, Henri is too little to understand . . .
The incessant gale force winds bring to mind my mortality.
I must act quickly. I am going to give the little twisted door
what it wants in order to save us. I kneel down in front of the
miniature door and I declare:

« to be = être
I am = je . . . »

Suddenly, there is a gust of wind so intense that it is
intolerable. I cover my face with my hands
in order to protect myself and then I hear the monstrous voice of the wind,

« HENRI . . . HENRI . . . HENRI! »

*I think (for) an instant and **finally** I understand!*
« That's it!
Henri, the wind is whistling your name in order to tell you that
it's up to YOU to make this twisted door open!
Not me!
*Your **existence**, your well-**being** are at stake! »*
Henri seems to understand. In turn,
he kneels down in front of the twisted door . . .
All of a sudden, it starts to get very cold.
We feel a vibration all around us.
*« Françoise, **what is this?** »*
Then we hear a demonic voice that resonates
like thunder:

« Ah, my little Henri! Françoise is wrong!
If you listen to her, you will both die! »

---

se **moq**uer de = to make fun of; to laugh at (think: **mock**)
heureusement = fortunately; luckily
* **heureux** = happy
comprendre = to understand (think: **compr**eh**end**)
vent soufflant (*or* vent qui souffle) en tempête = gale force winds
rappeler = to remind; to bring to mind
devoir = must
agir = to act
s'a**genou**iller = to **knee**l (down)
* le **genou** = the knee
devant = in front of
couv**r**ir = to **cover**
proté**ger** = to **prote**ct
la **voi**x = the **voi**ce
être en jeu = to be at stake
* un jeu = a game
avoir l'air = to seem; to look; to appear
il fait froid = it's cold (weather)
* il fait chaud = it's hot (weather)
* il fait du vent = it's windy
avoir tort = to be wrong
* avoir raison = to be right

In Chapitre 17, you learned that the expression **to be right** is **avoir raison** and that it conjugates with the verb **avoir**. The expression **to be wrong** is formed in exactly the same way: you just conjugate the verb **avoir** and then add the word **tort**. Get it?

Examples:
j'**ai tort** = I am wrong
nous **avons raison** = we are right

Avoir l'air means **to seem**; **to look**; **to appear**. You also form this expression in the same manner by conjugating the verb **avoir** and then adding the words **l'air**.

Examples:
j'**ai l'air** triste = I look sad
il **a l'air** heureux = he seems happy

Study hard and then take this test.

1. il a l'air petit = _____
2. il fait du vent = _____
3. happy = _____
4. the knee = _____
5. the voice = _____
6. in front of = _____
7. je me moque de vous = _____
8. it's cold (weather) = _____
9. il fait chaud = _____
10. I look big = _____
11. couvrir = _____
12. agir = _____
13. they appear happy = _____
14. you (plural) are wrong = _____
15. we are right = _____
16. you (singular, familiar) are right = _____

Voici les réponses:

1. he looks little
2. it's windy
3. heureux
4. le genou
5. la voix
6. devant
7. I make fun of you
8. il fait froid
9. it's hot (weather)
10. j'ai l'air grand
11. to cover
12. to act
13. ils ont l'air heureux
14. vous avez tort
15. nous avons raison
16. tu as raison

If you missed more than two on this test, you must
study and take the test again. Then, when you are
ready, you may go on to Chapitre 26 to find out
if little Henri listens to the diabolical voice!

NOTES

CHAPITRE VINGT-SIX 26

L'orage nous a trouvés. Nous sommes trempés jusqu'aux os.
Pour moi, les éclairs ressemblent à des lignes étroites entre
la vie et la mort. Mais pire encore, cette présence satanique
semble pénétrer chaque goutte d'eau, chaque coup de tonnerre.
Est-ce que nous allons nous en sortir?
« Henri! Je crois que j'ai raison! Tu dois faire ouvrir la porte tordue!
Tu dois le faire tout seul sans mon aide!
Il ne faut pas écouter cet être malfaisant! »
Henri ferme les yeux. Je le vois mordre sa lèvre inférieure.
Puis il avale. Il respire à fond, et avec un certain
courage, il commence à faire ce qu'il lui faut pour se sauver.

◈

The storm has found us. We are soaked to the bone (skin).
For me, the streaks of lightning resemble narrow lines between
life and death. But even worse, this satanical presence
seems to penetrate each drop of water, each clap of thunder.
Are we ever going to get out of this?
« Henri! I believe that I am right! You must make the twisted door open!
You have to do it all alone without my help!
You mustn't listen to this evil being! »
Henri closes his eyes. I see him bite his lower lip.
Then he swallows. He takes a deep breath, and with a certain (amount of)
courage, he commences to do what he must in order to save himself.

◈

être trempé jusqu'aux os = to be soaked to the bone (skin)
jusqu'à = (up) to; as far as; until
une **ligne** = a line
étroite = narrow (feminine)
entre = between
la **vi**e = the life (think: **vi**able)
pire = worse
chaque = each
eau = water
aller = to go
devoir = must; to have to
mordre = to bite
avaler = to swallow

Now you must learn the verb **aller**.
It is an irregular **-er** verb, so watch out!

Here goes:

aller = to go

je vais = I go; I am going; I do go
tu vas = you go; you are going; you do go
il, elle va = he, she, it goes; he is going; he does go
nous all**ons** = we go; we are going; we do go
vous all**ez** = you go; you are going; you do go
ils, elles vont = they go; they are going; they do go

Make the effort to learn this verb.
You might need it later. Get my drift?

Here is another irregular **-oir** verb that you have
seen many times with endings similar to
irregular **-ir** verbs: **devoir**

dev**oir** = must; to have to

je doi**s** = I must; I have to
tu doi**s** = you must; you have to
il, elle doi**t** = he, she, it must; he has to
nous dev**ons** = we must; we have to
vous dev**ez** = you must; you have to
ils, elles doiv**ent** = they must; they have to

Now take this test. Watch out. It's tricky!

1. he is going = _____
2. aller = _____
3. tu dois = _____
4. each = _____
5. water = _____
6. between = _____
7. I am going = _____
8. he does go = _____
9. vous devez = _____
10. you (singular, familiar) go = _____
11. je dois = _____
12. they do go = _____
13. the life = _____
14. a line = _____
15. narrow (masculine) = _____

Voici les réponses:

1. il va
2. to go
3. you must; you have to
4. chaque
5. eau
6. entre
7. je vais
8. il va
9. you must; you have to
10. tu vas
11. I must; I have to
12. ils vont or elles vont
13. la vie
14. une ligne
15. étroit

If you missed more than one, study and take the test over if you want to find out what poor Henri will do in the next chapter. Will he save himself? When you are ready, you may proceed to Chapitre 27.

Henri essaie de s'essuyer les yeux couverts de pluie,
mais c'est une bataille perdue d'avance.
La pluie torrentielle continue malgré ses efforts.
En effet, tout semble perdu.
Il s'agenouille devant la petite porte tordue.
La boue couvre ses petits genoux.
D'un air triste, il me regarde comme pour la dernière fois.
Je fais semblant de sourire pour lui donner du courage.
Puis il commence à haute voix:

« être = to be
je suis = I am
tu. . . tu. . . »

« **J'ai oublié, Françoise!** »
« **Tu peux le faire, Henri! Réfléchis!** »
Le temps semble une éternité. Mais Henri n'a pas l'air de
s'en souvenir!
Est-ce qu'il sera condamné le restant de ses jours?
Le vent se lève subitement. Il y a de nouveau une rafale
de vent très intense accompagnée d'un mugissement pétrifiant:

« es. . . es. . . **es!** »

Henri pousse un cri:
« **C'EST ÇA:**

tu **es** = you are
il est = he is
nous sommes = we are
vous êtes = you are
ils sont = they are**!** »

La petite porte tordue miniature s'ouvre
d'elle-même.

Henri tries to wipe his eyes covered with rain,
but it is a losing battle.
The torrential rain continues despite his efforts.
Indeed, everything seems lost.
He kneels down in front of the little twisted door.
Mud covers his little knees.
With an air of sadness, he looks at me as if for the last time.
I pretend to smile in order to give him courage.
Then he begins aloud:

« to be = être
I am = je suis
you . . . you . . . »

« I forgot, Françoise! »
« You can do it, Henri! Think! »
Time seems an eternity. But Henri does not look like
he remembers!
Will he be condemned for the rest of his days (life)?
The wind suddenly picks up. There is again a very intense gust
of wind accompanied by a petrifying howl,

*« are . . . are . . . **are!** »*

Henri lets out a cry,
« THAT'S IT:

*you **are** = tu es*
he is = il est
we are = nous sommes
you are = vous êtes
they are = ils sont! »

The little twisted miniature door opens
by itself.

essayer de = to try to
s'essuyer = to wipe oneself; to dry oneself
la pluie = the rain
une **bat**ai**lle** = a **bat**tle
sembler = to seem
perdu = lost (masculine)
la boue = the mud
comme = as (if); like
dernière = last (feminine)
fois = time
faire semblant = to pretend
sourire = to smile
lui = him
donner = to give (think: **don**ate)
à haute voix = aloud
haute = loud; high (feminine)
le temps = (the) time; the weather
le **jour** = the day (think: **jour**nal)
de **nouveau** = a**new**; again

Now, try learning these indirect object pronouns:
me; **te**; **lui**; **nous**; **vous**; **leur**

me = me
te = you (singular, familiar)
lui = him; her
nous = us
vous = you
leur = them

Here are examples using the **to give** verb **donner**.
Notice that *clé* is the *direct object* of the verb **donner**:

il **me** donne la clé = he gives **me** the key *or* he gives the key to **me**
je **te** donne la clé = I give **you** the key *or* I give the key to **you**
je **lui** donne la clé = I give **him** or **her** the key *or* I give the key to **him** or to **her**
elle **nous** donne la clé = she gives **us** the key *or* she gives the key to **us**
je **vous** donne la clé = I give **you** the key *or* I give the key to **you**
je **leur** donne la clé = I give **them** the key *or* I give the key to **them**

Did you notice that these indirect object
pronouns are placed *before* the verb **donner**?

90

Now study and take this test.

1. to give = _____
2. the battle = _____
3. to seem = _____
4. as; like = _____
5. the day = _____
6. the days = _____
7. (the) time; the weather = _____
8. the rain = _____
9. I give her the key = _____
10. I give them the key = _____
11. she gives me the key = _____
12. I give the key to you (singular, familiar) = _____
13. he gives the key to us = _____
14. I give you (plural) the key = _____
15. I give the key to him = _____

Voici les réponses:

1. donner
2. la bataille
3. sembler
4. comme
5. le jour
6. les jours
7. le temps
8. la pluie
9. je lui donne la clé
10. je leur donne la clé
11. elle me donne la clé
12. je te donne la clé
13. il nous donne la clé
14. je vous donne la clé
15. je lui donne la clé

If you missed more than one, you cannot
go on to the next chapter. Study and take the
test again if you want to find out in Chapitre 28
what happens when the little twisted door opens!

Aussitôt que la petite porte s'ouvre, nous ressentons
un tremblement de terre si fort que cela nous fait perdre l'équilibre.
Plouf!
Nous nous trouvons par terre complètement couverts de boue.
Henri essaie de se lever mais il glisse et se retrouve dans la boue.
Les tremblements s'arrêtent.
À ce moment-là, j'essaie de me lever quand je vois quelque chose d'étrange:
l'épaississement surréel de l'air devant moi.
D'abord, je discerne quelque chose de flou et grisâtre.
Puis cela prend forme.
Horrifiée, je me rends compte que c'est un être sinistre qui se réalise!
Je le reconnais. . . C'est le vieux monsieur qui se matérialise!
C'est vrai, alors. Le vieux monsieur est un fantôme!
Donc, la question obligatoire se pose:
pourquoi se sent-il obligé de nous révéler son secret?

*As soon as the little door opens, we feel
such a strong earthquake that it makes us lose our balance.
Splash!
We find ourselves on the ground completely covered in mud.
Henri tries to get up but he slips and finds himself again in the mud.
The tremors stop.
At that moment, I try to get up when I see something strange:
the surreal thickening of the air in front of me.
At first, I can make out something hazy and grayish.
Then it takes shape.
Horrified, I realize that it is a grim-looking being in the making!
I recognize him . . . It is the old gentleman who is materializing!*

It's true, then. The old gentleman is a ghost!
Therefore, the obligatory question arises:
why does he feel obligated to reveal his secret to us?

aussi**tôt** = as **soon** as
ressentir = to feel; to experience
si = so; such
perdre = to lose
plouf! = splash!
par **terre** = on the ground
la **terre** = the ground; the earth (think: extra**terre**strial; **terr**ain)
se lever = to get up
glisser = to slide; to slip
arrêter = to stop
épaissir = to thicken
d'abord = at first
flou = hazy; blurred
gris**âtre** = gray**ish**
* gris – gray
prendre = to take
un être = a being
reconnaître = to **recog**nize
c'est **vrai** = it is true
vrai = true
* c'est **faux** = it is wrong; it is untrue
* **faux** = **fa**lse
donc = therefore
se poser = to arise
pourquoi = why

Do you remember the endings for **-re** verbs?
You should! They are **-s**, **-s**, no ending, **-ons**, **-ez**, **-ent**.
Now try to conjugate **perdre** and then take this test.

1. flou = _____
2. on the ground = _____
3. it is true = _____
4. d'abord = _____
5. prendre = _____
6. so = _____
7. to slide = _____
8. grayish = _____

9. to recognize = _____

10. it is untrue = _____

11. why = _____

12. therefore = _____

Voici les réponses:

perd**re** = to lose

je perd**s** = I lose; I am losing; I do lose

tu perd**s** = you lose; you are losing; you do lose

il, elle perd = he, she, it loses; he is losing; he does lose

nous perd**ons** = we lose; we are losing; we do lose

vous perd**ez** = you lose; you are losing; you do lose

ils, elles perd**ent** = they lose; they are losing; they do lose

1. hazy; blurred
2. par terre
3. c'est vrai
4. at first
5. to take
6. si
7. glisser
8. grisâtre
9. reconnaître
10. c'est faux
11. pourquoi
12. donc

If you missed more than two, study and take the test over. Then when you are ready, you may go on to Chapitre 29 to find out what the phantom is up to!

NOTES

Les petits yeux noirs du fantôme se concentrent sur le petit Henri.
Avec un sourire sardonique et d'une voix encore plus basse
et sonore, le vieux monsieur lui prophétise:

« Ah! Henri, fais tes adieux à Françoise!
Donne-moi la main! »

« Non, Henri. Ne l'écoute pas! Je dois être sur
la bonne voie! **C'est pour cela qu'il s'est matérialisé!** »
J'entends un grognement épouvantable.
« Touche la petite porte tordue! »
Les tremblements de terre recommencent aussitôt,
mais le fantôme est dupé car ses astuces marchent moins
bien **sur des sujets qui sont déjà par terre!**
Henri profite de la situation:
toujours allongé par terre, il touche la petite porte
d'une main et tend l'autre main vers moi.
Je réagis très rapidement pour lui donner la main.
Un instant, nous faisons les maillons d'une chaîne humaine.
Je tourne la tête vers le haut pour regarder une dernière fois
le ciel orageux et je crie:
« Merci le Vent! »
Et la tempête s'arrête aussitôt.

The little black eyes of the phantom concentrate on little Henri.
With a sardonic smile and with an even lower
and resonant voice, the old gentleman prophesies,

« Ah! Henri, say farewell to Françoise!
Give me your hand! »

« No, Henri. Don't listen to him! I must be on
*the right track! **That's why he materialized!** »*
I hear a dreadful growl.
« Touch the little twisted door! »
The earthquakes immediately start over again,
but the phantom is fooled because his clever ways work less
*effectively **on subjects that are already on the ground!***
Henri takes advantage of the situation:
still lying on the ground, he touches the little door
with one hand and extends his other hand toward me.
I react very quickly to give him my hand.
(For) an instant, we form the links of a human chain.
I turn my head upwards to look one last time at
the stormy sky and I scream,
« Thank you, the Wind! »
And the storm immediately stops.

un sou**rire** = a smile
* sous = under
* un **rire** = a laugh
encore = again; even
basse = low (feminine)(think: **base**ment)
sonore = re**son**ant (think: **so**und)
* le **son** = the sound
écouter = to listen to
la voie = the track; the route
un **gro**gnement = a **gro**wl
épouvantable = dreadful
astuce = shrewdness; cleverness; clever way
marcher = to work
moins = less (think: **min**us)
les **sujet**s = the **subject**s
déjà = already
profiter **de** = to take advantage **of**
rapide**ment** = quick**ly**
un maillon = a link
le ciel = the sky; the heaven
orageux = **storm**y
* un **orage** = a (thunder)storm
merci = thank you

Now conjugate and translate the verb
profiter de. It is an **-er** verb. Then take this test.

1. un maillon = _____
2. a thunderstorm = _____
3. the sound = _____
4. a smile = _____
5. a laugh = _____
6. déjà = _____
7. la voie = _____
8. the sky = _____
9. again = _____
10. under = _____
11. un grognement = _____
12. thank you = _____

Voici les réponses:

profit**er** de = to take advantage of

je profit**e** de = I take advantage of; I am taking advantage of; I do take advantage of

tu profit**es** de = you take advantage of; you are taking advantage of; you do take advantage of

il, elle profit**e** de = he, she, it takes advantage of; he is taking advantage of; he does take advantage of

nous profit**ons** de = we take advantage of; we are taking advantage of; we do take advantage of

vous profit**ez** de = you take advantage of; you are taking advantage of; you do take advantage of

ils, elles profit**ent** de = they take advantage of; they are taking advantage of; they do take advantage of

1. a link
2. un orage
3. le son
4. un sourire
5. un rire
6. already
7. the track; the route
8. le ciel
9. encore
10. sous
11. a growl
12. merci

If you missed more than two, study and
take the test over if you want to find out what
awaits Henri and Françoise in Chapitre 30!

NOTES

Boum!
Nous nous retrouvons par terre dans la pièce au tableau vivant!
Nous avons réussi à sortir du cimetière!
Nous nous levons lentement. Malgré le choc, nous sommes
tout de suite attirés par la peinture vivante.
Henri se met devant moi pour étudier la peinture de plus près.
« Il n'y a rien de changé, Françoise, les portes tordues sont
toujours là », dit-il d'un air déçu.
À mon tour, j'analyse la peinture.
Je crains que le pauvre Henri n'ait raison.
Et puis je remarque quelque chose.
« Henri, regarde encore cette peinture à l'huile. Qu'est-ce que tu vois? »
« Je vois des portes tordues. »
« Maintenant, dis-moi ce que **tu ne vois pas**. »
Il me regarde d'un air perplexe.
Il réexamine la peinture. Ensuite, je le vois sauter en l'air.
« Je ne suis pas là! Je ne suis plus là! »
« Nous avons bien libéré ton esprit, Henri! » je crie à tue-tête.
Nous sautons de joie tous les deux ensemble
en faisant un boucan pas possible!
« Chut. . . ! »
« C'est toi qui as dit ça, Henri? »
« Mais non », répond-il un peu inquiet.
« J'ai pensé que c'était vous, Françoise. »
« Non, ce n'était pas moi. »

Bang!
We find ourselves back on the ground in the room with the living painting!
We succeeded in getting out of the cemetery!
We get up slowly. In spite of the shock, we are
immediately drawn to the living painting.
Henri puts himself in front of me in order to study the painting more closely.
« There is nothing changed, Françoise, the twisted doors are
still there, » he says with a disappointed look.
In turn, I analyze the picture.
I fear that poor Henri is right.
And then I notice something.
« Henri, look again at this oil painting. What do you see? »
« I see some twisted doors. »
« Now, tell me what **you don't see***. »*
He looks at me with a perplexed air.
He re-examines the painting. Then, I see him jump up in the air.
« I am not there! I am no longer there! »
« We really freed your spirit, Henri! » I shout at the top of my voice.
We both jump for joy together
while making an impossible racket!
« Shhh . . . ! »
« Did you say that, Henri? »
« Of course not, » he answers a little worried.
« I thought that it was you, Françoise. »
« No, it wasn't me. »

boum! = bang!; boom!
réussir = to succeed
se lever = to get up
lente**ment** = slow**ly**
tout de suite = immediately
attirer par = to be attracted to; to be drawn to
étudier = to **stud**y
rien = nothing
toujours = **al**ways; forever; still
déçu = disappointed (masculine)
à mon **tour** = in **tur**n
remarquer = to notice
hu**il**e = o**il**
maintenant = now
ensuite = afterwards; then
sauter = to jump
ensemble = together
chut! = shhh!
inquiet = worried (masculine)
penser = to think

Now you must learn how to say the following:
I succeed; **I do not succeed**; **I do not succeed any more**;
I succeed at nothing; **I only succeed**; **I never succeed**

Remember in Chapitre 8 you learned to put
ne and **pas** around the verb to make it negative?
This is very similar. Watch this!

je réussis = I succeed

ne. . . **pas** = not
je **ne** réussis **pas** = I do **not** succeed

ne. . . **plus** = not . . . any more
je **ne** réussis **plus** = I do **not** succeed **any more**

ne. . . **rien** = nothing (not anything)
je **ne** réussis **rien** = I succeed at **nothing**

ne. . . **que** = only
je **ne** réussis **que** = I **only** succeed

ne. . . **jamais** = never (not ever)
je **ne** réussis **jamais** = I **never** succeed

And speaking of succeeding, we have finally found an
example of the conjugation of a regular **-ir** verb!
You will see that it is slightly different from the
irregular **-ir** verbs that you have learned!
The endings to regular **-ir** verbs are
-is, -is, -it, -issons, -issez, -issent.

réuss**ir** = to succeed

je réuss**is** = I succeed; I do succeed; I am succeeding
tu réuss**is** = you succeed; you are succeeding; you do succeed
il, elle réuss**it** = he, she succeeds; he is succeeding; he does succeed
nous réuss**issons** = we succeed; we are succeeding; we do succeed
vous réuss**issez** = you succeed; you are succeeding; you do succeed
ils, elles réuss**issent** = they succeed; they are succeeding; they do succeed

Get it? You had better look all this over
before this little test. However, you might really
need it later for a much more important reason!

Now take this test.

1. nothing = _____
2. plus = _____
3. I never succeed = _____
4. you (singular, familiar) do not succeed any more = _____
5. ensemble = _____
6. tout de suite = _____
7. we succeed at nothing = _____
8. you (plural) do not succeed = _____
9. to study = _____
10. se lever = _____
11. to notice = _____
12. always = _____
13. I only succeed = _____
14. huile = _____
15. sauter = _____
16. afterwards = _____

Voici les réponses:

1. rien
2. more
3. je ne réussis jamais
4. tu ne réussis plus
5. together
6. immediately
7. nous ne réussissons rien
8. vous ne réussissez pas
9. étudier
10. to get up
11. remarquer
12. toujours
13. je ne réussis que
14. oil
15. to jump
16. ensuite

If you missed more than two, study and take
the test over. Be well prepared. This is a warning!
When you are ready, you may go on to Chapitre 31.

« Si ce n'est pas moi, et ce n'est pas toi, qui a dit 'chut'? »
« Je ne sais pas. Il n'y a que vous, moi, et cette peinture
dans la pièce. »
« Bon, c'est sans doute un son sans signification. Toutes ces
vieilles maisons ont de petits bruits de grincement ou de craquement,
n'est-ce pas, Henri? »
« Non. »
« Pourquoi dis-tu 'non'? »
« Je n'ai pas dit 'non'. »
« Comment ça tu n'as pas dit 'non'? »
« Je vous dis que je n'ai pas dit 'non'. »
« Henri. Ce n'est pas le moment de te moquer de moi. »
« Je ne me moque pas de vous. »
« Mais si. Je commence à me fâcher. »
« Pourquoi vous fâchez-vous? Je n'ai rien fait. »
« Mais si. Tu dis que tu n'as pas dit 'non'. »
« Je n'ai pas dit 'non'. »
« Comment ça tu n'as pas dit 'non'? »
« Je vous dis que je n'ai. . . »
« Arrêtez! »
« Qui a dit ça? »
« Pas moi. »
« Ohhhh, on ne va pas tout recommencer! »
« Ça c'est vrai! » *dit la peinture.*

◈

« If it's not me, and it's not you, who said 'shhh'? »
« I don't know. There's only you, me, and this painting
in the room. »
« All right, it's no doubt a sound without significance. All these
old houses have little noises of creaking or squeaking,
don't they, Henri? »
« No. »
« Why are you saying 'no'? »
« I didn't say 'no.' »
« What do you mean you didn't say 'no'? »
« I'm telling you that I did not say 'no.' »
« Henri. This is no time to poke fun at me. »
« I'm not poking fun at you. »
« Sure, (you are). I'm starting to get angry. »
« Why are you getting angry? I haven't done anything. »
« But of course, (you have). You are saying that you did not say 'no.' »
« I didn't say 'no.' »

« What do you mean you didn't say 'no'? »
« I'm telling you that I did not . . . »
« Stop! »
« Who said that? »
« Not me. »
« Ohhhh, we're not going to start all over again! »
« That's true! » says the painting.

moi = me
toi = you
il **n**'y a **que** = there is **only**
bon = good; all right
* jour = day
* bonjour = hello
sans = without
le doute = the doubt
le bruit = the noise
un grincement = a creaking
un craquement = a creaking; a squeaking
n'est-ce pas? = isn't it (so)?; don't you think?
pourquoi = why
se fâcher = to get angry
recommencer = to start (over) again; to begin again

You are going to learn **to say** the verb **dire**.
It is irregular. Watch out for the **vous** form!
No **ez** ending to be found!

dire = to say; to tell

je di**s** = I say; I am saying; I do say
tu di**s** = you say; you are saying; you do say
il, elle di**t** = he, she, it says; he is saying; he does say
nous dis**ons** = we say; we are saying; we do say
vous dites = you say; you are saying; you do say
ils, elles dis**ent** = they say; they are saying; they do say

Now you need to learn how to say **I said**.
I said, **I have said**, and **I did say** are **j'ai dit**. This
is called the *passé composé* because it is a compound
past tense formed with an auxiliary verb: **avoir** or **être**.
To form the passé composé of the verb **dire**, all you do is
conjugate the present indicative of **avoir** and then you
add a past participle which in this case is **dit**. That's
it. Study the conjugation of the past tense of **dire**:

j'**ai** dit = I said; I have said; I did say
tu **as** dit = you said; you have said; you did say
il **a** dit = he said; he has said; he did say
nous **avons** dit = we said; we have said; we did say
vous **avez** dit = you said; you have said; you did say
ils **ont** dit = they said; they have said; they did say

Clear? If you need to, review the conjugation of
avoir which is in bold letters. Then take this little test.
Hint: No tricks. The whole test will be about **said**.

1. you (singular, familiar) said = _____
2. he said = _____
3. j'ai dit = _____
4. we said = _____
5. ils ont dit = _____
6. you (plural) said = _____
7. she did say = _____
8. I did say = _____
9. they said = _____

Voici les réponses:

1. tu as dit
2. il a dit
3. I said; I did say
4. nous avons dit
5. they said; they did say
6. vous avez dit
7. elle a dit
8. j'ai dit
9. ils ont dit or elles ont dit

You have seen that it is not too difficult to form the
passé composé once you know the past participle that you
must use. So, here are the rules for forming the passé composé
and determining the past participle for **-er**, **-ir**, and **-re** verbs:
First you conjugate the present indicative of **avoir** (some verbs
have to be conjugated with **être** instead) and then you add
the past participle which is formed in the following way:

For **-er** verbs, take the **root** of the infinitive (**parl**er) and add an **é**.
So, the past participle is **parlé**.
Example: we spoke = nous avons parlé

For **-ir** verbs, take the **root** of the infinitive (**rempl**ir) and add an **i**.
So, the past participle is **rempli**.
Example: they filled = ils ont rempli

For **-re** verbs, take the **root** of the infinitive (**entend**re) and add a **u**.
So, the past participle is **entendu**.
Example: you heard = tu as entendu

But beware!
You will encounter verbs (like **dire** and **faire**)
that do not obey these exact rules!

■

Ready for one more complication?
What if you want to say, **I did not say**.
You are going to put **ne** and **pas** around the verb **avoir**.
The past participle **dit** is not touched! Watch this:

je **n**'ai **pas** dit = I did not say
tu **n**'as **pas** dit = you did not say
il **n**'a **pas** dit = hc did not say
nous **n**'avons **pas** dit = we did not say
vous **n**'avez **pas** dit = you did not say
ils **n**'ont **pas** dit = they did not say

Got it?
By the way, have you wondered why the **ne** turned into **n'**?
That's simply because some big guy decided that it didn't
sound very nice to say two vowel sounds in a row as in
« Je n**e a**i pas dit. »
He (or she?) said to throw out the '**e**' in n**e** and
put an apostrophe in its place. And so it was.
That's also why **I have** is **j'ai** and not **je ai**!

■

Now, instead of a big test, go back and study this chapter.
See how many times you can find and say aloud
je n'ai pas dit and **tu n'as pas dit**!
When you are done, you may go on to Chapitre 32!

Cette peinture a vraiment parlé!
Nous nous regardons.
« Ah! » crie Henri.
Nous courons tous les deux vers la porte pour échapper à
la peinture parlante quand nous entendons:

Les portes tordues sont dans la maison
Passez par elles pour sortir.
Mais l'air ne fait pas la chanson
Mes enfants,
Elles sont dures à trouver, il faut le dire.

La voix douce et pourtant résolue de la peinture
me met à l'aise. J'ai peut-être tort, mais j'ai l'impression
qu'elle ne nous pose pas de danger.
« Henri, attends. Je ne crois pas que cette peinture
soit méchante. Au contraire, j'ai l'impression
qu'elle veut nous aider. As-tu entendu ce qu'elle a dit?
Il faut passer par les portes tordues pour
sortir de la maison! »
Henri n'est toujours pas rassuré. Il reste toujours collé
à la porte de sortie.
« Je reste là. On ne sait jamais. On doit prendre
ses précautions », dit-il d'une voix affaiblie.
« D'ailleurs, il n'y a pas de portes tordues dans la
maison sauf dans le cimetière et dans la *peinture elle-même!*
Cette peinture parlante est peut-être une ruse du fantôme! »
« Écoute, Henri. Moi aussi, j'ai peur. Mais nécessité fait loi.
La peinture est notre seul recours! »
Henri soupire.
« D'accord. Admettons que ce n'est pas une ruse
du fantôme et que les portes tordues existent
dans la maison. Comment pouvons-nous les trouver? »
Henri me regarde d'un air ironique:
« Nous pouvons toujours demander au fantôme! »
« Parfois tu m'agaces! Pourtant, ton idée n'est pas
si bête que ça. »
« Qu'est-ce que vous voulez dire, Françoise? » dit-il perplexe.
« Nous pouvons poser la question à la peinture! »
Sans attendre de réponse d'Henri (je pense que c'est
mieux ainsi), j'avance vers la peinture à l'huile.
« Jolie peinture, où sont-elles les portes tordues? »
Je saute quand elle me répond:

Elles sont là
Où tu n'entrerais pas!

This painting really spoke!
We look at each other.
« Ah! » cries out Henri.
We both run toward the door to escape from
the talking painting when we hear:

The twisted doors are in the house
Go through them to get out.
But you can't judge a book by its cover
My children,
They are hard to find, it must be said.

The sweet and yet resolute voice of the painting
puts me at ease. I am perhaps wrong, but I have the impression
that it doesn't pose any danger to us.
« Henri, wait. I don't believe that this painting
is wicked. On the contrary, I have the impression
that it wants to help us. Did you hear what it said?
We have to go through the twisted doors in order
to get out of the house*! »*
Henri is still not reassured. He still stays glued
to the exit door.
« I'm staying here. One never knows. One has to take
precautions, » he says with a feeble voice.
« Besides, there are no twisted doors in the
house except in the cemetery and in the painting itself!
This talking painting is perhaps a trick by the phantom! »
« Listen, Henri. I'm scared too. But beggars can't be choosers.
The painting is our only recourse! »
Henri sighs.
« O.K. Let's assume that it isn't a trick
by the phantom and that the twisted doors exist
in the house. How can we find them? »
Henri looks at me with an ironic air:
« We can always ask the phantom! »
« Sometimes you irritate me! Nevertheless, your idea is not
as stupid as all that. »
« What do you mean, Françoise? » he says perplexed.
« We can ask the painting. »
Without waiting for Henri's answer (I think that it is
better this way), I walk toward the oil painting.
« Pretty painting, where are the twisted doors? »
I jump when it answers me:

They are there
Where you would not enter!

vrai**ment** = real**ly**; tru**ly**
parler = to speak; to talk
entendre = to hear
passer par = to go through
l'air = the tune; the air
la chan**son** = the **son**g
« l'air ne fait pas la chanson » = « you can't judge a book by its cover »
dur = hard (think: **dur**able)(masculine)
croire = to believe
au **contra**ire = on the **contrar**y
avoir l'impression = to have the feeling or impression
rester = to stay
d'ailleurs = besides; moreover
il **n**'y a **pas** = there is **not**; there are **not**
* il y a = there is; there are
une ruse = a ruse; a trick
aussi = too; also
« nécessité fait loi » = « beggars can't be choosers »
soupirer = to sigh
d'accord = all right; O.K.; agreed
bête = stupid
* la **bêt**e = the **be**a**st**
mieux = better
ainsi = thus; in this way

How do you think you would conjugate the present tense and
the passé composé of **parler**? No hints. Try it yourself now.

How do think you would say, **I have not spoken**?
Don't forget: **Spoke**, **have spoken**, and **did speak**
are the same words in French! Again, no hints.

How would you say, **I did not speak any more**?

Now, answer the above questions and then take this test!

1. the song = _____
2. soupirer = _____
3. hard = _____
4. croire = _____
5. d'ailleurs = _____
6. a trick = _____
7. il n'y a pas = _____
8. on the contrary = _____
9. to hear = _____
10. he has the impression = _____

110

parl**er** = to speak; to talk
je parl**e** = I speak; I am speaking; I do speak
tu parl**es** = you speak; you are speaking; you do speak
il, elle parl**e** = he, she, it speaks; he is speaking; he does speak
nous parl**ons** = we speak; we are speaking; we do speak
vous parl**ez** = you speak; you are speaking; you do speak
ils, elles parl**ent** = they speak; they are speaking; they do speak

j'**ai** parlé = I spoke; I have spoken; I did speak
tu **as** parlé = you spoke; you have spoken; you did speak
il, elle **a** parlé = he, she, it spoke; he has spoken; he did speak
nous **avons** parlé = we spoke; we have spoken; we did speak
vous **avez** parlé = you spoke; you have spoken; you did speak
ils, elles **ont** parlé = they spoke; they have spoken; they did speak

I have **not** spoken = je **n**'ai **pas** parlé
I did **not** speak **any more** = je **n**'ai **plus** parlé

1. la chanson
2. to sigh
3. dur
4. to believe
5. besides; moreover
6. une ruse
7. there is not; there are not
8. au contraire
9. entendre
10. il a l'impression

If you missed more than three, study and take the
entire test over. If you need to, slow down and take
your time. It is always better to do a good job slowly
than a bad job quickly! Your work will pay off later,
if you get my meaning! When you are ready to find
out what the speaking painting's riddles mean,
you may go on to Chapitre 33.

Je ne m'attendais pas à ce que la peinture réponde!
J'essaie de me calmer.
Toujours un peu essoufflée, je répète les devinettes:

L'air ne fait pas la chanson

**Elles sont là
Où tu n'entrerais pas**

« Ce sont des énigmes, Henri. Je n'y comprends rien. »
Henri ne me répond pas. En ouvrant très doucement
la porte de la pièce, il jette un coup d'œil sur l'embrasure de la porte.
Personne. Le couloir est vide.
Nous y entrons pour trouver un couloir bien étrange.
Il y a des ombres et des lumières qui semblent danser
le long des murs et des portes en bois.
Mais il y a un illogisme:
il n'y aucune source apparente pour
ces lumières qui sautillent.
Subitement, les lumières cessent leur danse. Puis,
elles s'éteignent. Le couloir se noircit et se remplit d'une
présence terrible et horrifiante.
« **Ah, vous êtes là mes enfants!** »
sa voix résonne comme le tonnerre.
« Vite, Henri, cours! Sauve-toi!
Pousse la porte en bois devant toi! »
Mais le petit Henri se retourne pour faire face à son ennemi. . .
Il prend sa course, non pas vers la porte en bois pour se sauver,

mais vers la présence elle-même!
« Non, Henri! Arrête! » je crie à tue-tête.
Mais il persiste dans sa poursuite vers ce danger mortel.
« Vous voyez vos dernières heures! »
crie le spectre.
Puis j'entends un cri épouvantable. Silence.
« Henri! Henri! Qu'est-ce que tu as fait, mon pauvre Henri?! »
Sans réfléchir, je me trouve en train de courir vers
l'être malfaisant.
Même si je meurs, je dois essayer de sauver le petit Henri.
Je vois la grande présence devant moi.
Elle est noirâtre et semble remplir tout le couloir.
Je ferme les yeux et je saute vers elle. . .

I wasn't expecting that the painting would answer!
I try to calm myself.
Still a little out of breath, I repeat the riddles:

You can't judge a book by its cover

They are there
Where you would not enter

« These are riddles, Henri. I don't understand a thing. »
Henri doesn't answer me. While opening very gently
the door to the room, he casts a glance upon the doorway.
Nobody. The hall is empty.
We enter to find a very strange hallway.
There are shadows and lights that seem to dance
along the walls and wooden doors.
But there is an illogicality:
there is no apparent source for
these lights that jump about.
Suddenly, the lights cease their dance. Then,
they go out. The hall blackens and fills with a
terrible and horrifying presence.
« Ah, you are there my children! »
his voice resonates like thunder.
« Quick, Henri, run! Save yourself!
Push on the wooden door in front of you! »
But little Henri turns around to face his enemy . . .
He starts running, not toward the wooden door to save himself,

but toward the presence itself!
« No, Henri! Stop! » I yell at the top of my voice.
But he persists in his pursuit toward (this) mortal danger.
*« **You are seeing your last hours!** »*
cries out the specter.
Then I hear a dreadful cry. Silence.
« Henri! Henri! What have you done, my poor Henri?! »
Without thinking, I find myself running toward
the evil being.
Even if I die, I must try to save little Henri.
I see the large presence in front of me.
It is blackish and seems to fill the entire hallway.
I close my eyes and I jump toward it . . .

s'attendre à = to expect
une **devine**tte = a riddle
* **deviner** = to guess
comprendre = to understand
jeter = to throw; to cast
un coup d'**œil** = a glance
œil = eye
embrasure de la porte = doorway
personne = no one; nobody
un couloir = a hall(way) (US); a corridor
une ombre = a shadow
un mur = a wall (think: **mur**al)
sautiller = to jump about
* **saut**er = to jump
noircir = to blacken
remplir = to fill
un **en**n**em**i = an **enem**y
prendre sa course = to start running
* prendre = to take
essayer de = to try to
noir**âtre** = black**ish**

Now learn how to conjugate the irregular
verbs **prendre** and **comprendre**. They are **-re** verbs
with identical endings. But notice that the letter **d**
disappears in the **nous**, **vous**, and **ils** forms,
while the **n** doubles in the **ils** form.

114

prend**re** = to take

je prend**s** = I take; I am taking; I do take
tu prend**s** = you take; you are taking; you do take
il, elle prend = he, she, it takes; he is taking; he does take
nous pren**ons** = we take; we are taking; we do take
vous pren**ez** = you take; you are taking; you do take
ils, elles prenn**ent** = they take; they are taking; they do take

comprend**re** = to understand

je comprend**s** = I understand; I am understanding; I do understand
tu comprend**s** = you understand; you are understanding; you do understand
il, elle comprend = he, she, it understands; he is understanding; he does understand
nous compren**ons** = we understand; we are understanding; we do understand
vous compren**ez** = you understand; you are understanding; you do understand
ils, elles comprenn**ent** = they understand; they are understanding; they do understand

If **fait** is the past participle or *participe passé* of the verb **faire**,
how do you think you would conjugate the passé composé of this verb?

What are the participes passés of the verbs **attendre**, **réfléchir**, and **essayer**?
No hints! Answer these questions now and then take the test below.

1. a riddle = _____
2. noircir = _____
3. you (singular, polite) do understand = _____
4. un coup d'œil = _____
5. we are taking = _____
6. I do understand = _____
7. I am taking = _____
8. a hall(way); a corridor = _____
9. she understands = _____
10. he is taking = _____
11. remplir = _____
12. blackish = _____
13. we do understand = _____
14. a wall = _____
15. they understand (masculine) = _____
16. jeter = _____

Voici les réponses:

j'**ai** fait = I did; I have done
tu **as** fait = you did; you have done
il, elle **a** fait = he, she, it did; he, she, it has done
nous **avons** fait = we did; we have done
vous **avez** fait = you did; you have done
ils, elles **ont** fait = they did; they have done

The participe passé of attend**re** is attend**u**.
The participe passé of réfléch**ir** is réfléch**i**.
The participe passé of essay**er** is essay**é**.

1. une devinette
2. to blacken
3. vous comprenez
4. a glance
5. nous prenons
6. je comprends
7. je prends
8. un couloir
9. elle comprend
10. il prend
11. to fill
12. noirâtre
13. nous comprenons
14. un mur
15. ils comprennent
16. to throw; to cast

Wait!
Before you check to see how many you missed,
you must look into the future, the future tense that is!

The rules are the same for both **-er** and **-ir** verbs.
Take the whole infinitive such as **entrer** or **sortir**.
Then add the following endings:
-ai, -as, -a, -ons, -ez, -ont
Example: I will enter = j'entrer**ai**

For **-re** verbs,
you must first drop the **e** before adding these same endings.
Example: Take prend**re**. Drop the **e** so that it is now **prendr**,
and then add the appropriate ending.
Example: we will take = nous prendr**ons**

116

So if you really want to get out of this chapter, study this example of the conjugation of the future tense of **sortir**:

je sortir**ai** = I will go out
tu sortir**as** = you will go out
il sortir**a** = he will go out
nous sortir**ons** = we will go out
vous sortir**ez** = you will go out
ils sortir**ont** = they will go out

Now, if you missed more than two on
the test, study well and take the test over.
Then when you are ready, you may proceed to
Chapitre 34 if you want to find out what the future
holds for Françoise as she tries to save poor Henri!

NOTES

J'ouvre les yeux. Je respire. . . Je dois être en vie.
Je vois mal. . . Tout est flou, grisâtre.
Je tends la main.
Je touche quelque chose de doux et chaud.
« Françoise? » murmure-t-il.
« Henri? C'est toi? Tu vas bien? »
Le flou commence à se dissiper.
La figure d'Henri prend la place du flou.
« Henri! Ça va? Qu'est-ce que tu as fait? »
« J'ai réfléchi, Françoise. . . j'ai réfléchi aux devinettes. »
« Comment? »
« Vous m'avez toujours dit de réfléchir, n'est-ce pas? »
« Oui, mais. . . c'est absurde. Maintenant nous sommes
piégés à l'intérieur d'un fantôme! »
Henri apparaît calme.
« Non, Françoise. Je ne pense pas qu'on soit piégé
Regardez là-bas, un peu plus loin »,
dit-il en montrant du doigt.
En effet, *c'est une porte tordue!*

I open my eyes. I am breathing . . . I must be alive.
I see poorly . . . Everything is blurred, grayish.
I hold out my hand.
I touch something soft and warm.
« Françoise? » he murmurs.
« Henri? Is it you? Are you all right? »
The blurriness starts to dissipate.
Henri's face takes the place of the fuzziness.
« Henri! Are you O.K.? What did you do? »
« I thought, Françoise . . . I thought about the riddles. »
« What? »
« You always did tell me to think, didn't you? »
« Yes, but . . . this is absurd. Now we are
trapped inside a ghost! »
Henri appears calm.
« No, Françoise. I don't think that we are trapped.
Look over there, a little farther down, »
he says while pointing.
Indeed, it is a twisted door!

ouvrir = to open
respirer = to breathe
en vie = alive
doux = soft; sweet; mild (masculine)
chaud = warm; hot (masculine)
tu vas bien? = are you all right?
le flou = the fuzziness; the blurriness
comment = how; what
oui = yes
piéger = to trap
un peu = a little
plus = more
loin = far
plus loin = farther
montrant du doigt = pointing
* montrer = to show; to point to

Do you remember in Chapitre 26 you learned
how to conjugate the **to go** verb, **aller**?
This same verb is used in the following expression:
How are you?

Watch this:

comment **allez-vous**? = how **are you**?
comment **vas-tu**? = how **are you**? (singular and familiar)

The answers to these questions are the following:

je vais bien = I am fine; I am well; I am all right
je vais mal = I am doing poorly

Now review the conjugation of **aller**.
By just adding **bien** or **mal**, a
fine expression is formed!

je **vais** bien = I am fine
tu **vas** bien = you are fine
il **va** bien = he is fine
nous **allons** bien = we are fine
vous **allez** bien = you are fine
ils **vont** bien = they are fine

Now take this test.

1. to open = _____
2. warm = _____
3. how are you (singular, familiar)? = _____
4. he is fine = _____
5. alive = _____
6. they are fine (feminine) = _____
7. how are you (plural)? = _____
8. I am fine = _____
9. we are doing poorly = _____
10. far = _____
11. farther = _____
12. a little = _____
13. I am doing poorly = _____

Voici les réponses:

1. ouvrir
2. chaud
3. comment vas-tu?
4. il va bien
5. en vie
6. elles vont bien
7. comment allez-vous?
8. je vais bien
9. nous allons mal
10. loin
11. plus loin
12. un peu
13. je vais mal

If you missed more than one, study and take the
test over. Then when you are ready, you may go
on to Chapitre 35 to discover the secrets of
the twisted door found inside the ghost!

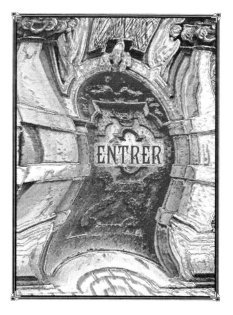

On se regarde avec joie.
« Henri, tu es génial! »
Le petit Henri sourit modestement.
Nous avançons lentement vers la porte tordue.
Elle est très bizarre, en bois, grande, les bords tordus
ainsi que le reste de la porte elle-même. Même le cadre autour
de la porte est tordu. Logiquement, elle
ne devrait pas exister, et pourtant elle est là devant nous.
Curieuse de savoir, **je pose la main sur elle**.
Aussitôt, des lettres dorées entourées d'un genre
d'auréole apparaissent sur la porte pour créer le mot suivant:

ENTRER

We look at each other with joy.
« Henri, you're a genius! »
Little Henri smiles modestly.
We walk slowly toward the twisted door.
It is very bizarre, wooden, big, the edges twisted
as well as the rest of the door itself. Even the frame around
the door is twisted. Logically, it
should not exist, and yet it is there in front of us.
*Curious (to know), **I place my hand on it**.*
***Immediately**, golden letters surrounded by a type*
of halo appear on the door so as to create the following words:

TO ENTER

Can you help conjugate this verb for Françoise?
You must do it for her if you want to find out what
happens in the next chapter. Deal?

Voici les réponses:

entrer = to enter
j'entre = I enter
tu entres = you enter
il, elle entre = he, she, it enters
nous entrons = we enter
vous entrez = you enter
ils, elles entrent = they enter

If you missed even one, you cannot proceed to the
next chapter and the door will not open for Françoise!
So study until you can fulfill the twisted door's demands!
When you have made no mistakes, you may go
on to Chapitre 36. A little word of warning:
Danger lurks behind one of the doors!

La porte tordue s'ouvre toute seule. . .
« Entrons, Henri. »
Nous entrons par la porte tordue. Immédiatement, elle
se ferme derrière nous avec le bruit d'une porte qui est très lourde.
« Françoise, regardez ce qui est devant nous! »
« Eh bien, une autre porte tordue! »
Henri pose sa petite main sur cette nouvelle porte tordue.
Aussitôt, des lettres dorées entourées d'un genre
d'auréole apparaissent sur la porte pour créer les mots suivants:

ÊTRE

AVOIR

The twisted door opens all by itself . . .
« Let's enter, Henri. »
We enter by way of the twisted door. Immediately, it
closes behind us with the sound of a door that is very heavy.
« Françoise, look at what is in front of us! »
« Well, another twisted door! »
Henri places his little hand on this new twisted door.
Immediately, golden letters surrounded by a type
of halo appear on the door so as to create the following words:

TO BE

TO HAVE

Can you help Henri conjugate these two verbs?
His fate is in your hands!

Voici les réponses:

être = to be
je suis = I am
tu es = you are
il, elle est = he, she, it is
nous sommes = we are
vous êtes = you are
ils, elles sont = they are

avoir = to have
j'ai = I have
tu as = you have
il, elle a = he, she, it has
nous avons = we have
vous avez = you have
ils, elles ont = they have

If you missed even one, the door
will not open for Henri! So study until
you can fulfill the twisted door's demands!
When you have made no mistakes, you may go
on to Chapitre 37. A little word of warning:
Danger lurks behind one of the doors!

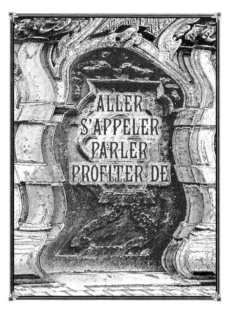

La porte tordue s'ouvre toute seule. . .
« Entrons, Françoise. »
Nous entrons par la porte tordue. Immédiatement, elle
se ferme derrière nous avec le bruit d'une porte qui est très lourde.
« Henri, regarde ce qui est devant nous! »
« Eh bien, une autre porte tordue! »
Je pose la main sur cette nouvelle porte tordue.
Aussitôt, des lettres dorées entourées d'un genre
d'auréole apparaissent sur la porte pour créer les mots suivants:

ALLER
S'APPELER
PARLER
PROFITER DE

The twisted door opens all by itself . . .
« Let's enter, Françoise. »
We enter by way of the twisted door. Immediately, it
closes behind us with the sound of a door that is very heavy.
« Henri, look at what is in front of us! »
« Well, another twisted door! »
I place my hand on this new twisted door.
Immediately, golden letters surrounded by a type
of halo appear on the door so as to create the following words:

TO GO
TO CALL ONESELF (NAME)
TO SPEAK
TO TAKE ADVANTAGE OF

Can you help Françoise conjugate these verbs?
Her fate is in your hands!

Voici les réponses:

aller = to go
je vais = I go
tu vas = you go
il, elle va = he, she, it goes
nous allons = we go
vous allez = you go
ils, elles vont = they go

s'appeler = to call oneself
je m'appelle = my name is
tu t'appelles = your name is
il, elle s'appelle = his, her, its name is
nous nous appelons = our names are
vous vous appelez = your name(s) is (are)
ils, elles s'appellent = their names are

parler = to speak
je parle = I speak
tu parles = you speak
il, elle parle = he, she, it speaks
nous parlons = we speak
vous parlez = you speak
ils, elles parlent = they speak

profiter de = to take advantage of
je profite de = I take advantage of
tu profites de = you take advantage of
il, elle profite de = he, she, it takes advantage of
nous profitons de = we take advantage of
vous profitez de = you take advantage of
ils, elles profitent de = they take advantage of

If you missed even one, the door
will not open for Françoise! So study until
you can fulfill the twisted door's demands!
When you have made no mistakes, you may go
on to Chapitre 38. A little word of warning:
Danger lurks behind one of the doors!

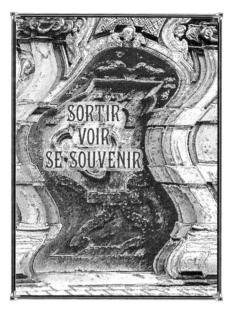

La porte tordue s'ouvre toute seule. . .
« Entrons, Henri. »
Nous entrons par la porte tordue. Immédiatement, elle
se ferme derrière nous avec le bruit d'une porte qui est très lourde.
« Françoise, regardez ce qui est devant nous! »
« Eh bien, une autre porte tordue! »
Henri pose sa petite main sur cette nouvelle porte tordue.
Aussitôt, des lettres dorées entourées d'un genre
d'auréole apparaissent sur la porte pour créer les mots suivants:

SORTIR
VOIR
SE SOUVENIR

The twisted door opens all by itself . . .
« Let's enter, Henri. »
We enter by way of the twisted door. Immediately, it
closes behind us with the sound of a door that is very heavy.
« Françoise, look at what is in front of us! »
« Well, another twisted door! »
Henri places his little hand on this new twisted door.
Immediately, golden letters surrounded by a type
of halo appear on the door so as to create the following words:

TO GO OUT (TO LEAVE)
TO SEE
TO REMEMBER

Can you help Henri conjugate these verbs?
His fate is in your hands!

Voici les réponses:

sortir = to go out; to leave
je sors = I go out
tu sors = you go out
il, elle sort = he, she, it goes out
nous sortons = we go out
vous sortez = you go out
ils, elles sortent = they go out

voir = to see
je vois = I see
tu vois = you see
il, elle, voit = he, she, it sees
nous voyons = we see
vous voyez = you see
ils, elles voient = they see

se souvenir = to remember
je me souviens = I remember
tu te souviens = you remember
il, elle, se souvient = he, she, it remembers
nous nous souvenons = we remember
vous vous souvenez = you remember
ils, elles se souviennent = they remember

If you missed even one, the door
will not open for Henri! So study until
you can fulfill the twisted door's demands!
When you have made no mistakes, you may go
on to Chapitre 39. A little word of warning:
Danger lurks behind one of the doors!

La porte tordue s'ouvre toute seule. . .
« Entrons, Françoise. »
Nous entrons par la porte tordue. Immédiatement, elle
se ferme derrière nous avec le bruit d'une porte qui est très lourde.
« Henri, regarde ce qui est devant nous! »
« Eh bien, une autre porte tordue! »
Je pose la main sur cette nouvelle porte tordue.
Aussitôt, des lettres dorées entourées d'un genre
d'auréole apparaissent sur la porte pour créer les mots suivants:

FAIRE
IL FAIT CHAUD
FAIT (participe passé)

The twisted door opens all by itself . . .
« Let's enter, Françoise. »
We enter by way of the twisted door. Immediately, it
closes behind us with the sound of a door that is very heavy.
« Henri, look at what is in front of us! »
« Well, another twisted door! »
I place my hand on this new twisted door.
Immediately, golden letters surrounded by a type
of halo appear on the door so as to create the following words:

TO DO
IT IS HOT (WEATHER)
DONE (past participle)

Can you help Françoise with these words?
Her fate is in your hands!

First, conjugate the verb **faire** for Françoise.
Then give the answers to the following:

1. it is hot (weather) = _____
2. it is cold = _____
3. it's windy = _____
4. I have done = _____
5. you (singular, familiar) did = _____
6. he did = _____
7. we have done = _____
8. they did (masculine) = _____
9. you (plural) did = _____
10. she has done = _____

Voici les réponses:

faire = to do; to make
je fais = I do
tu fais = you do
il, elle fait = he, she, it does
nous faisons = we do
vous faites = you do
ils, elles font = they do

1. il fait chaud
2. il fait froid
3. il fait du vent
4. j'ai fait
5. tu as fait
6. il a fait
7. nous avons fait
8. ils ont fait
9. vous avez fait
10. elle a fait

If you missed even one, the door
will not open for Françoise! So study until
you can fulfill the twisted door's demands!
When you have made no mistakes, you may go
on to Chapitre 40. A little word of warning:
Danger lurks behind one of the doors!

La porte tordue s'ouvre toute seule. . .
« Entrons, Henri. »
Nous entrons par la porte tordue. Immédiatement, elle
se ferme derrière nous avec le bruit d'une porte qui est très lourde.
« Françoise, regardez ce qui est devant nous! »
« Eh bien, une autre porte tordue! »
Henri pose sa petite main sur cette nouvelle porte tordue.
Aussitôt, des lettres dorées entourées d'un genre
d'auréole apparaissent sur la porte pour créer les mots suivants:

LE VOCABULAIRE

The twisted door opens all by itself . . .
« Let's enter, Henri. »
We enter by way of the twisted door. Immediately, it
closes behind us with the sound of a door that is very heavy.
« Françoise, look at what is in front of us! »
« Well, another twisted door! »
Henri places his little hand on this new twisted door.
Immediately, golden letters surrounded by a type
of halo appear on the door so as to create the following word:

VOCABULARY

Can you help Henri with these words or expressions?
His fate is in your hands!

1. around = _____
2. partout = _____
3. an eye = _____
4. tout de suite = _____
5. the eyes = _____
6. like; as = _____
7. bien = _____
8. more = _____
9. presque = _____
10. the head = _____
11. une devinette = _____
12. far = _____
13. surtout = _____
14. the stone = _____
15. puis = _____
16. sous = _____
17. trouver = _____
18. the forehead = _____
19. déjà = _____
20. despite = _____

Voici les réponses:

1. autour
2. everywhere
3. un œil
4. immediately
5. les yeux
6. comme
7. well
8. plus
9. almost; nearly
10. la tête
11. a riddle
12. loin
13. especially
14. la pierre
15. then
16. under
17. to find
18. le front
19. already
20. malgré

If you missed even one, the door
will not open for Henri! So study until
you can fulfill the twisted door's demands!
When you have made no mistakes, you may go
on to Chapitre 41. A little word of warning:
Danger lurks behind one of the doors!

La porte tordue s'ouvre toute seule. . .
« Entrons, Françoise. »
Nous entrons par la porte tordue. Immédiatement, elle
se ferme derrière nous avec le bruit d'une porte qui est très lourde.
« Henri, regarde ce qui est devant nous! »
« Eh bien, une autre porte tordue! »
Je pose la main sur cette nouvelle porte tordue.
Aussitôt, des lettres dorées entourées d'un genre
d'auréole apparaissent sur la porte pour créer le mot suivant:

DIVERS

The twisted door opens all by itself . . .
« Let's enter, Françoise. »
We enter by way of the twisted door. Immediately, it
closes behind us with the sound of a door that is very heavy.
« Henri, look at what is in front of us! »
« Well, another twisted door! »
I place my hand on this new twisted door.
Immediately, golden letters surrounded by a type
of halo appear on the door so as to create the following word:

DIVERSE

Can you help Françoise with these words and expressions?
Her fate is in your hands!

1. it is me (I) = _____
2. I do not speak any more = _____
3. he said = _____
4. a hit; a blow = _____
5. better = _____
6. near = _____
7. it is necessary to answer = _____
8. a light = _____
9. the pain = _____
10. am I a boy? = _____
11. pouvons-nous? = _____
12. qu'est-ce que c'est? = _____
13. to read = _____
14. quelqu'un = _____
15. se moquer de = _____
16. happy = _____
17. we spoke = _____
18. devant = _____
19. the voice = _____
20. entre = _____

Voici les réponses:

1. c'est moi
2. je ne parle plus
3. il a dit
4. un coup
5. mieux
6. près
7. il faut répondre
8. une lumière
9. la douleur
10. est-ce que je suis un garçon?
11. can we?
12. what is it?; what is this?
13. lire
14. someone; somebody
15. to make fun of
16. heureux
17. nous avons parlé
18. in front of
19. la voix
20. between

If you missed even one, the door
will not open for Françoise! So study until
you can fulfill the twisted door's demands!
When you have made no mistakes, you may go
on to Chapitre 42. A little word of warning:
Danger lurks behind one of the doors!

La porte tordue s'ouvre toute seule. . .
« Entrons, Henri. »
Nous entrons par la porte tordue. Immédiatement, elle
se ferme derrière nous avec le bruit d'une porte qui est très lourde.
« Françoise, regardez ce qui est devant nous! »
« Eh bien, une autre porte tordue! »
Henri pose sa petite main sur cette nouvelle porte tordue.
Aussitôt, des lettres dorées entourées d'un genre
d'auréole apparaissent sur la porte pour créer les mots suivants:

LE VOCABULAIRE

The twisted door opens all by itself . . .
« Let's enter, Henri. »
We enter by way of the twisted door. Immediately, it
closes behind us with the sound of a door that is very heavy.
« Françoise, look at what is in front of us! »
« Well, another twisted door! »
Henri places his little hand on this new twisted door.
Immediately, golden letters surrounded by a type
of halo appear on the door so as to create the following word:

VOCABULARY

Can you help Henri with these words?
His fate is in your hands!

1. la vie = _____
2. l'eau = _____
3. chaque = _____
4. the rain = _____
5. a smile = _____
6. (the) time; the weather = _____
7. a day = _____
8. donc = _____
9. why = _____
10. it is true = _____
11. again = _____
12. thank you = _____
13. now = _____
14. together = _____
15. who = _____
16. hello = _____
17. the song = _____
18. on the contrary = _____
19. d'accord = _____
20. thus; in this way = _____

Voici les réponses:

1. the life
2. the water
3. each
4. la pluie
5. un sourire
6. le temps
7. un jour
8. therefore
9. pourquoi
10. c'est vrai
11. encore; de nouveau
12. merci
13. maintenant
14. ensemble
15. qui
16. bonjour
17. la chanson
18. au contraire
19. all right; O.K.; agreed
20. ainsi

If you missed even one, the door
will not open for Henri! So study until
you can fulfill the twisted door's demands!
When you have made no mistakes, you may go
on to Chapitre 43. A little word of warning:
Danger lurks behind one of the doors!

La porte tordue s'ouvre toute seule. . .
« Entrons, Françoise. »
Nous entrons par la porte tordue. Immédiatement, elle
se ferme derrière nous avec le bruit d'une porte qui est très lourde.
« Henri, regarde ce qui est devant nous! »
« Eh bien, une autre porte tordue! »
Je pose la main sur cette nouvelle porte tordue.
Aussitôt, des lettres dorées entourées d'un genre
d'auréole apparaissent sur la porte pour créer les mots suivants:

LE VOCABULAIRE

The twisted door opens all by itself . . .
« Let's enter, Françoise. »
We enter by way of the twisted door. Immediately, it
closes behind us with the sound of a door that is very heavy.
« Henri, look at what is in front of us! »
« Well, another twisted door! »
I place my hand on this new twisted door.
Immediately, golden letters surrounded by a type
of halo appear on the door so as to create the following word:

VOCABULARY

Can you help Françoise with these words or expressions?
Her fate is in your hands!

1. en effet = _____
2. ouvrir = _____
3. être en train de = _____
4. to lose = _____
5. astuce = _____
6. in = _____
7. inside = _____
8. depuis = _____
9. to put = _____
10. yet; nevertheless = _____
11. a thunderstorm = _____
12. essayer de = _____
13. against = _____
14. méchant = _____
15. tous les deux = _____
16. là-bas = _____
17. la clé = _____
18. to cry = _____
19. réfléchir = _____
20. outside = _____

Voici les réponses:

1. indeed
2. to open
3. to be in the process of
4. perdre
5. shrewdness; cleverness; clever way
6. dans; en
7. dedans
8. since; for
9. mettre; poser
10. pourtant
11. un orage
12. to try to
13. contre
14. wicked
15. both
16. over there
17. the key
18. pleurer
19. to think
20. dehors

If you missed even one, the door
will not open for Françoise! So study until
you can fulfill the twisted door's demands!
When you have made no mistakes, you may go
on to Chapitre 44. A little word of warning:
Danger lurks behind one of the doors!

NOTES

« Françoise, je suis fatigué. Nous sommes passés
par au moins huit portes tordues.
Est-ce que cela va finir? »
« Henri, il faut avoir du courage. N'oublie pas que la jolie
peinture nous a dit de passer par les portes tordues.
Nous n'avons pas le choix. Nous devons essayer de
faire ce qu'elle nous a dit. »
Il soupire. . .

Henri avance de nouveau vers une porte tordue.
Dès qu'il arrive sur le seuil de la porte, nous voyons
qu'elle n'est pas comme les autres:
un visage surnaturel à traits illuminés apparaît subitement
sur la porte tordue! Les petits
yeux noirs pénétrants nous fixent jusqu'à l'âme.
La bouche énorme, encadrant un espace noir infini,
articule les mots suivants:

**« Vous n'allez jamais sortir d'ici, mes enfants.
Vous êtes à moi! »**

déclare le spectre à voix si tonitruante que les
vibrations font secouer le couloir.

Henri est figé par la peur devant la porte tordue.
Le fantôme en profite:
une grande main à bras long qui semble naître
de la surface de la porte empoigne le pauvre Henri. . .
La main fantomatique tient le petit corps d'Henri
comme un étau tout en **l'éloignant de la porte**.
« Françoise! Au secours! »
Je cours vers Henri pour l'aider. Arrivée à son côté, une chose néfaste
se passe: je perds l'équilibre et tombe par terre.
Je tends la main en désespoir de cause vers Henri
qui essaie de donner de grands coups de pied pour se libérer.
Ces mouvements distraient l'apparition un moment.
Je réussis à passer la main entre les pieds d'Henri
et à **toucher** ainsi la partie inférieure de la porte tordue.
L'apparition pousse un cri qui semble provenir de l'enfer.
Mais il tient Henri encore plus fort!
Tout à coup, des lettres dorées entourées d'un genre
d'auréole se superposent au front affreux du fantôme
pour créer le mot suivant:

SORTIR

« Mon Dieu! J'ai trop peur pour me souvenir
comment conjuguer **SORTIR**! Au secours! »

« Françoise, I'm tired. We have gone
through at least eight twisted doors.
Is this going to end? »
« Henri, you have to be brave. Don't forget that the pretty
painting told us to go through the twisted doors.
We have no choice. We must try
to do what it told us. »
He sighs . . .

◈

Henri moves on again toward a twisted door.
As soon as he arrives on the door's threshold, we see
that it is not like the others:
A supernatural face with illuminated features suddenly appears
on *the twisted door! The little*
black penetrating eyes stare at us to the very soul.
The enormous mouth, framing a black infinite space,
articulates the following words:

*« **You are never going to get out of here, my children.***
***You are mine!** »*

declares the specter with such a thunderous voice that the
vibrations make the hall shake.
Henri is terror-stricken in front of the twisted door.
The phantom takes advantage of this:
A large hand with a long arm seeming to arise
from the surface of the door grabs poor Henri . . .
The ghostly hand holds little Henri's body
*in a viselike grip while **moving him away from the door**.*
« Françoise! Help! »
I run toward Henri to help him. Reaching his side, an ill-fated thing
happens: I lose my balance and fall to the ground.
I extend my hand in sheer desperation toward Henri
who is trying to kick himself free.
These movements distract the apparition (for) a moment.
I manage to pass my hand between Henri's feet
*and to thereby **touch** the bottom part of the twisted door.*
The apparition lets out a cry that seems to come from hell.
But he holds Henri even tighter!
Suddenly, golden letters surrounded by a type
of halo superimpose themselves on the hideous forehead of the phantom
so as to create the following words:

TO GO OUT

« My goodness! I'm too afraid to remember
*how to conjugate **TO GO OUT**! Help! »*

Can you help conjugate **SORTIR** for Françoise?
If not, Françoise and Henri will be prisoners in this
terrible house forever!

Voici les réponses:

sortir = to go out
je sors
tu sors
il, elle sort
nous sortons
vous sortez
ils, elles sortent

If you missed even one, Françoise and Henri are doomed!
You must study and get it right for their sake!
When you have made no mistakes,
you may go on to Chapitre 45 . . .
if you dare!

NOTES

Je me lève rapidement. Grâce à l'aide d'un
bon samaritain, je me souviens de la conjugaison
du verbe, **SORTIR**!

Je récite:

sortir = to go out
je sors
tu sors
il, elle sort
nous sortons
vous sortez
ils, elles sortent

J'entends aussitôt un hurlement abominable:
« **Ahhhhh!!** »
La bouche déjà énorme du fantôme s'élargit pour révéler
un espace noir infini et macabre.
C'est évident que l'intention du spectre est de nous avaler!
Or, la porte tordue s'ouvre. . .

I get up quickly. Thanks to the help of a
good Samaritan, I remember the conjugation
*of the verb, **TO GO OUT**!*

I recite:

to go out = sortir
I go out
you go out
he, she goes out
we go out
you go out
they go out

I immediately hear an abominable howl,
« ***Ahhhhh!!*** »
The already enormous mouth of the phantom widens to reveal
a black, infinite, macabre space.
It is obvious that the specter's intention is to swallow us!
Now, the twisted door opens . . .

NOTES

Ça sent bon. . . L'air frais. La lumière. . .
La lumière naturelle. . .
Je suis dehors. Je suis sortie de la maison!
Quelle honte!
Pendant quelques secondes, j'ai oublié mon pauvre Henri.
Quelle fin atroce!
Il a été sans doute avalé par le fantôme. . .
Je commence à pleurer.
« Mon pauvre Henri. Je suis si malheureuse.
Tu me manques! »
« Vous me manquez aussi! »
Je lève les yeux pour voir devant moi le petit
Henri sain et sauf!
Nous nous embrassons très fort.
« Françoise, maintenant j'ai une petite surprise pour vous. »
Je me retourne.
« Merci Françoise! » disent-**ils**.
« Françoise, j'ai le grand honneur de vous présenter
mes parents, Monsieur et Madame Woodward. »
« Françoise, vous nous avez tous sauvés. »
« Enchantée, mais je regrette, je n'y comprends rien. »
« Mais si », dit Monsieur Woodward.
« Cependant, je vous ai aidée un tout petit peu aussi », dit-il en riant.
Je suis complètement confuse.
« Vous vous souvenez du vent? »

« Oui, bien sûr. Grâce au vent, nous avons réussi
à sortir du cimetière. »
Monsieur Woodward déclare:
« C'était moi le vent! »
« Et c'était moi la 'jolie peinture', comme vous dites »,
affirme Madame Woodward.
Madame Woodward continue son discours:
« Nous étions tous captifs dans la maison de ce fantôme méchant.
Le spectre nous a transformés pour que nous ne puissions pas
aider Henri. Entre autres, le fantôme a effacé
de sa mémoire tout ce qui concernait notre existence. »
Je l'interromps:
« J'ai trouvé curieux qu'il ne parle jamais de ses parents. »
« Oui », reprend Madame Woodward,
« ainsi, Henri ne pouvait pas nous chercher. »
« Le fantôme a sûrement pensé que nous étions tous
captifs pour l'éternité. Il n'aurait jamais pu s'imaginer
qu'une petite fille comme vous vienne nous sauver!
C'était là sa plus grande erreur!
Sinon, il vous aurait transformée aussi. »
« Et nous serions toujours dans cette maison! » dis-je en tremblant.
Madame Woodward me prend dans ses bras.
« Ne vous en faites pas, Françoise, vous êtes saine et sauve. »
Reprenant courage, je dis:
« Monsieur Woodward, Madame Woodward, et mon petit Henri,
maintenant je dois rentrer chez moi. . . Mes parents doivent
être très inquiets. Ils ne vont jamais me croire
quand je leur expliquerai que j'étais dans une maison hantée! »
« **Tant pis!** »
« Qui a dit ça? »
« Pas moi! »
« Moi non plus! »
« Ni moi! »
« Ohhhh, on ne va pas tout recommencer! »

It smells good . . . Fresh air. Light . . .
Natural light . . .
I am outside. I got out of the house!
How shameful!
For a few seconds, I forgot about my poor Henri.
What an atrocious end!
He was no doubt swallowed by the phantom . . .
I start to cry.
« My poor Henri. I am so unhappy.
I miss you! »
« I miss you too! »
I raise my eyes to see in front of me little
Henri safe and sound!
We kiss and hug each other very tightly.
« Françoise, now I have a little surprise for you. »
I turn around.
« Thank you, Françoise! » **they** *say.*
« Françoise, I have the great honor of presenting to you
my parents, Mr. and Mrs. Woodward. »
« Françoise, you saved us all. »
« Pleased to meet you, but I am sorry, I don't understand a thing. »
« Sure, (you do), » says Mr. Woodward.
« However, I helped you a little bit also, » he says while laughing.
I am completely confused.
« Do you remember the wind? »
« Yes, of course. Thanks to the wind, we succeeded
in getting out of the cemetery. »
Mr. Woodward declares,
« It was I, the wind! »
« And it was I the 'pretty painting,' as you say, »
asserts Mrs. Woodward.
Mrs. Woodward continues her discourse:
« We were all captives in the house by this wicked phantom.
The specter transformed us so that we could not
help Henri. Among other things, the phantom erased
from his memory everything concerning our existence. »
I interrupt her:
« I found it odd that he never spoke of his parents. »
« Yes, » resumes Mrs. Woodward,
« this way Henri couldn't look for us. »
« The phantom surely thought that we were all
captives for eternity. He could never have imagined
that a little girl like you would come to save us!
That was his biggest mistake!
Otherwise, he would have transformed you too. »
« And we would still be in that house! » I say trembling.

Mrs. Woodward takes me in her arms.
« Don't worry, Françoise, you are safe and sound. »
Regaining my courage, I say,
« Mr. Woodward, Mrs. Woodward, and my little Henri,
now I must go home . . . My parents must
be very worried. They are never going to believe me
when I explain to them that I was in a haunted house! »
*« **Too bad!** »*
« Who said that? »
« Not me! »
« Me neither! »
« Nor I! »
« Ohhhh, we're not going to start all over again! »

~~ LE VOCABULAIRE ~~

Key: *m* = masculine; *f* = feminine; *s* = singular; *pl* = plural; *adj* = adjective;
( ) = contents precede the entry in the story; numeral = chapter number

à = at; to, 7
accrocher = to hang (up), 13
adieu *m* = farewell; goodbye, 29
admettre = to admit; to assume, 32
affaiblir = to weaken, 32
affreux = hideous, 44
agacer = to irritate, 32
agenouiller (s') = to kneel (down), 25
agir = to act, 25
aider = to help, 22
aïe! = ouch!, 11
aimer = to like; to love, 19
ainsi = thus; in this way, 32
air *m* = tune; air; look, 19
aise (à l') = at ease, 32
aller = to go, 26, 34
allongé *m,s adj* = lying, 29
allons (nous) = we go (See *aller*), 26
alors = then, 4
âme *f* = soul, 44
à peine = barely; hardly, 24
apercevoir = to see; to perceive, 18
apparaître = to appear, 34
apparition *f* = apparition; specter, 44
appeler (s') = to call oneself, 6
approcher de (s') = to come up to, 17
appuyer = to press, 23
après = after, 11
arrêter = to stop, 28
arriver = to arrive, 3
assez = quite; enough, 19
astuce *f* = shrewdness; cleverness;
    clever way, 29
atroce = atrocious, 46
attendre = to wait (for), 19
attendre à (s') = to expect, 33
attirer = to attract, 19
au = to the, 7
au contraire = on the contrary, 32

aucune *f,s adj* = no; not any, 33
auréole *f* = halo, 35
aussi = too; also, 32
aussitôt = as soon as; immediately, 28
autour = around, 19
autre = other, 19
aux = to the, 7
avaler = to swallow, 26
avancer = to move forward, 2
avec = with, 5
avoir = to have, 2
avoir envie de = to feel like, 18
avoir l'air = to seem; to look, 25
avoir l'impression = to have the
    feeling, 32
avoir raison = to be right, 17
avoir tort = to be wrong, 25

baisser = to lower, 20
basse *f,s adj* = low, 29
bataille *f* = battle, 27
beaucoup = a lot; (very) much, 17
beaucoup de = many; a lot of, 6
bête *adj* = stupid, 32
bête *f* = beast, 32
bien = well, 14, 34
bien plus = much more, 20
bien sûr = of course, 46
blanc *m,s adj* = white, 14
blanche *f,s adj* = white, 18
bleu *m,s adj* = blue, 18
bloquer = to block (up), 16
bois *m* = wood, 6
bon = good, 31
bonjour = hello, 31
bord *m* = edge, 35
boucan *m* = racket, 30
bouche *f* = mouth, 20

boue *f* = mud, 27
bouger = to move, 7
boum! = bang!; boom!, 30
bout *m* = end; tip, 23
bras *m* = arm, 20
bruit *m* = noise; sound, 7
brun *m,s adj* = brown, 18

c' = Abbreviation of *ce*, 10
ça = that; it (Familiar for *cela*), 9
cacher = to hide, 22
cadre *m* = frame, 35
ça me dit quelque chose = that rings a
    bell; that reminds me of something,
    16
ça me fait mal = that hurts (me) (See
    faire mal), 11
captif *m* = captive, 46
car = because, 21
ça veut dire = that means; it means,
    17
ça y est = that's it, 10
ce *m,s adj* = this; that, 11
cela = that; it (See *ça*), 15
ce n'est pas = that is not, 14
cependant = however, 46
ces *m,f,pl adj* = these; those, 11
ce sont = these are, 33
cesser = to cease; to stop, 33
c'est = it is; that is, 10
c'est-à-dire = that is to say, 17
c'est faux = it is wrong, 28
c'est moi = it is me, 15
c'est toi = it is you, 15
c'est vrai = it is true, 28
cet *m,s adj* = this; that (Before a vowel
    or silent *h*), 11
cette *f,s adj* = this; that, 11
chagrin *m* = sorrow; grief, 23
chanson *f* = song, 32
chaque = each, 26
chaud = warm; hot, 25
chercher = to look for, 46
cheveux *m,pl* = hair, 20
chez moi = my place; my home, 46

choix *m* = choice, 44
chuchoter = to whisper, 20
chut! = shhh!, 30
ciel *m* = sky; heaven, 29
cinq = five, 3
clé *f* = key; clue, 24
cœur *m* = heart, 10
colle *f* = glue, 11
collé *m,s adj* = stuck, 11
comme = like; as (if); how, 27
commencer = to begin; to start, 8
comment = how; what, 34
comment allez-vous? = how are you?,
    34
comment se fait-il que? = how is it
    that?; how come?, 15
comment vas-tu? = how are you?, 34
comprendre = to understand, 33
compter = to count, 5
conjugaison *f* = conjugation, 45
conjuguer = to conjugate, 44
contre = against, 24
corps = body, 18
côté *m* = side, 23
couler = to flow; to run, 15
couloir *m* = hall(way); corridor, 11
coup *m* = hit; knock; blow, 23
coup de vent = gust of wind, 23
coup d'œil = glance, 33
couper le souffle (me) = to knock the
    breath out of me, 23
courage *m* = courage; bravery, 21
courir = to run, 11
courons (nous) = we run (See *courir*),
    11
course *f* = running, 33
court (il) = he runs (See *courir*), 11
couvrir = to cover, 21
craindre = to fear, 30
craquement *m* = creaking; squeaking,
    31
créer = to create, 35
crier à tue-tête = to shout one's head
    off; to shout or yell at the top of
    one's voice, 33
croire = to believe; to think, 10

d'abord = at first, 28
d'accord = all right; O.K.; agreed, 32
d'ailleurs = besides; moreover, 32
dans = in, 7
de = of; from; any; with; some, 7
debout = standing (up), 24
découvrir = to discover; to find out, 24
déçu *m,s adj* = disappointed, 30
dedans = inside, 15
déguisée *f,s adj* = disguised, 23
déguisement *m* = disguise, 23
dehors = outside, 18
déjà = already, 22
de la = from the; of the; some, 7
de nouveau = anew; again, 27
dépêcher (se) = to hurry (up), 23
depuis = since; for, 15
dernier *m,s adj* = last, 16
dernière *f,s adj* = last, 27
derrière = behind, 7
des = from the; of the; some, 7
désespoir de cause = sheer
    desperation, 44
dès que = as soon as, 44
destin *m* = destiny, 23
deux = two, 3
devant = in front of, 25
devenir = to become, 15
devient (il) = he becomes (See *devenir*),
    15
deviner = to guess, 33
devinette *f* = riddle, 33
devoir = must; to have to, 26
dire = to say; to tell, 31
discours *m* = speech; discourse, 46
dissiper (se) = to wear off, 34
distraire = to distract, 44
dit (il) = he says (See *dire*), 31
dix = ten, 3
doigt *m* = finger, 5
donc = therefore, 9
donner = to give, 27
dorées *f,pl adj* = golden, 35
douce *f,s adj* = soft; sweet; mild, 32
doucement = gently, 20
douleur *f* = pain, 23
doute *m* = doubt, 31

doux *m adj* = soft; sweet; mild, 34
du = from the; of the; some, 7
duper = to fool, 29
dur *m,s adj* = hard, 32

eau *f* = water, 26
éblouissante *f,s adj* = dazzling, 23
échapper = to escape, 16
éclair *m* = flash, streak of lightning,
    24
éclat *m* = burst, 24
écouter = to listen to, 29
écrit = written, 9
effacer = to erase, 46
effectivement = indeed, 9
effrayée *f,s adj* = frightened, 18
effroyable = horrifying, 21
eh bien = well, 36
élargir (s') = to widen itself, 45
elle *f* = she; it, 1
elle est = she is; it is, 1
elle-même = herself; itself, 23
elles *f,pl* = they, 1
éloigner = to move away, 44
embrasser = to kiss; to embrace, 46
embrasure de la porte = doorway, 33
empoigner = to grab (hold of), 44
en = in; to; of it; from it; made of, 6
en arrière = backwards, 21
encadrant = framing, 44
encore = again; even, 29
en effet = indeed, 14
enfant *m,f,s* = child, 12
enfants *pl* = children, 12
enfin = finally, 23
énigme *f* = riddle, 33
en jeu (être) = to be at stake, 25
enlever = to remove, 21
ennemi *m* = enemy, 33
en plus = what's more; besides, 10
ensemble = together, 16
ensuite = afterwards; then, 30
entendre = to hear, 22
entourées de *f,pl adj* = surrounded
    by, 35
en train de = in the process of, 12

entre = between, 26
entrer = to enter, 35
envahir = to invade; to overcome, 22
épaissir = to thicken, 28
épaule *f* = shoulder, 20
épeler = to spell (out), 24
épouvantable = dreadful, 29
erreur *f* = error, 46
espace *m* = space, 44
espoir *m* = hope, 16
esprit *m* = spirit; mind, 22
essayer de = to try to, 16
essoufflée (être) = to be out of breath, 33
est-ce que? = is it that?, 15
et = and, 3
étant = being, 18
étau *m* = vise, 44
éteindre = to extinguish, 33
étourdie *f,s adj* = dizzy, 23
étrange *s adj* = strange, 17
être = to be, 1
être *m* = being, 28
être en train de = to be in the process of, 14
étroit *m,s adj* = narrow, 26
étudier = to study, 30
évident *m,s adj* = obvious; evident, 22
exiger = to demand, 12

façon *f* = way, 23
façonner = to make; to fashion, 23
faire = to do; to make, 19
faire le ménage = to do the housework, 21
faire mal = to hurt, 11
faire semblant = to pretend, 27
fantomatique *adj* = ghostly, 44
fantôme *m* = ghost; phantom, 8
fatigué *m,s adj* = tired, 44
faux = false, 28
fermer = to close, 7
figer par la peur = to be terror-stricken, 44
figure *f* = face, 25
fille *f* = girl, 2

fin *f* = end, 18
finir = to end, 44
fixer = to fix, 44
flou *m* = fuzziness; blurriness, 34
flou *m,s adj* = blurred; hazy, 28
fois *f* = time, 27
fond (à) = deeply; in depth, 26
fort = hard; loud(ly); strong, 9
frais = fresh; cool, 46
franchement = frankly, 18
frappe (je) = I knock (See *frapper*), 3
frapper = to knock, 3
frissonner = to shiver, 22
froid = cold, 25
front *m* = forehead, 22

garçon *m* = boy, 10
gâté *m,s adj* = spoiled, 19
génial *m,s adj* = of genius, 35
genou *m* = knee, 25
genre *m* = type; sort, 35
glisser = to slide; to slip, 28
goutte *f* = drop, 22
grâce à = thanks to, 45
grand *m,s adj* = tall; big; large, 3
grande *f,s adj* = tall; big; large, 1
graver = to engrave, 23
grincement *m* = creaking, 31
gris *m adj* = gray, 18
grisâtre = grayish, 28
grognement *m* = growl, 29

habillé *m,s adj* = dressed, 14
habituer à (s') = to get use to, 17
hantée *f,s adj* = haunted, 46
haute *f,s adj* = high; loud, 27
haute voix (à) = aloud, 27
heure *f* = hour, 12
heureusement = fortunately; luckily, 25
heureux *m adj* = happy, 25
homme *m* = man, 3
honte *f* = shame, 46
huile *f* = oil, 30
huit = eight, 3

hurlement *m* = howl, 45

ici = here, 23
idée *f* = idea, 32
il *m* = he; it, 1
il a envie de pleurer = he feels like
    crying, 18
il fait chaud = it's hot (weather), 25
il fait du vent = it's windy, 25
il fait froid = it's cold (weather), 25
il faut = it is necessary, 23
il n'y a pas = there is (are) not, 32
il n'y a que = there is (are) only, 31
ils *m,pl* = they, 1
il y a = there is; there are, 21
inférieure *f,s adj* = lower; bottom, 20
inquiet *m,s adj* = worried, 30
inscrire = to inscribe; to engrave, 22

j'ai = I have, 2
j'ai envie de = I feel like, 18
jamais (ne. . .) = never, 30
jambe *f* = leg, 20
j'arrive = I arrive; I am coming, 3
jaune = yellow, 18
je = I, 1
je me suis fait mal = I hurt myself, 13
je ne peux pas = I cannot, 8
je ne suis pas = I am not, 8
je ne vois pas = I do not see, 17
je ne vois rien = I do not see anything,
    17
jeter = to throw, 33
jeu *m* = game (See *en jeu*), 25
joie *f* = joy, 30
jolie *f,s adj* = pretty, 44
joue *f* = cheek, 20
jour *m* = day, 27
jusqu'à = (up) to; all the way to, 26

la = the, 7
là = there, 15
là-bas = over there, 17
là-dedans = in(side) there, 15

laid *m,s adj* = ugly, 6
laissez-moi = let me, 7
lancer = to throw, 18
larmes *f,pl* = tears, 15
le = the, 7
le long de = along, 15
lentement = slowly, 5
les = the, 7
leur = them; their, 27
lever (se) = to get up, 23
lèvre *f* = lip, 20
ligne *f* = line, 26
lire = to read, 24
loin = far, 34
lourde *f,s adj* = heavy, 36
lui = him; her, 27
lumière *f* = light, 23

ma *f,s adj* = my, 8
maillon *m* = link, 29
main *f* = hand, 20
maintenant = now, 30
mais = but, 8
mais non = (but) of course not;
    I should think not, 8
maison *f* = house, 1
mal = bad(ly); poorly (See *faire mal*),
    24
malfaisant *m,s adj* = evil, 33
malgré = despite; in spite of, 22
malheureux *m adj* = unhappy, 18
manquer = to miss, 24
marcher = to work; to walk, 29
marron = brown, 18
me = me; myself, 6, 27
méchant *m,s adj* = wicked; mean, 16
même = same; even, 23
ménage *m* = housework, 21
merci = thank you, 29
mes *m,f,pl adj* = my, 10
mettre = to put, 24
mettre debout (se) = to stand up, 24
meurs (je) = I die (See *mourir*), 33
mieux = better, 32
mignon *m,s adj* = cute, 15
mince = thin, 24

moi = me, 7
moi aussi = me too, 13
moi-même = myself, 18
moi non plus = me neither, 12
moins = less, 29
mon *m,s adj* = my, 10
monde *m* = world, 22
monsieur = gentleman; sir, 12
montrant du doigt = pointing, 34
montrer = to show, 34
mordre = to bite, 26
mort *m,s adj* = dead, 22
mot *m* = word, 21
mourir = to die, 24
mugissement *m* = howl, 27
mur *m* = wall, 13

naître = to be born; to arise, 44
nécessité fait loi = beggars can't be
    choosers, 32
néfaste = ill-fated, 44
ne. . . jamais = never, 30
ne. . . pas = not, 30
ne. . . plus = any more, 30
ne. . . que = only, 30
ne. . . rien = nothing, 30
n'est-ce pas? = isn't it (so)?, 31
nettement = clearly, 21
neuf = nine, 3
nez *m* = nose, 20
ni. . . ni = neither . . . nor, 22
noir *m,s adj* = black, 3
noirâtre = blackish, 33
noircir = to blacken, 33
nom *m* = name, 18
non = no, 8
notre = our, 16
nous = we; us; ourselves, 6, 27
nous-mêmes = ourselves, 24
nouveau = new, 27
nouvelle *f,s adj* = new, 36
nuage *m* = cloud, 18

objet *m* = object, 23
obtenir = to obtain; to get, 20

œil *m* = eye, 19
ombre *f* = shadow, 33
on = one; we; you; they, 19
or = now; but; yet, 45
orage *m* = thunderstorm, 22
orageux = stormy, 29
orange = orange, 18
oreille *f* = ear, 20
os *m,s,pl* = bone(s), 26
ou = or, 24
où = where, 13
oublier = to forget, 23
oui = yes, 34
où sommes-nous? = where are we?,
    13
ouvrir = to open, 14

par = by; by way of; through, 19
parfois = sometimes, 32
parler = to speak; to talk, 32
parole *f* = word, 22
par terre = on the ground, 28
partout = everywhere, 19
pas (ne. . .) = not, 30
pas *m* = step, 18
pas moi = not me, 25
passer (se) = to happen, 44
passer par = to go through, 32
pauvre = poor, 17
peinture *f* = painting, 13
peinture à l'huile = oil painting, 13
pencher (se) = to lean over, 23
pendant = during; for, 46
penser = to think, 30
percevoir = to perceive, 18
perdre = to lose, 28
perdu *m,s adj* = lost, 27
personne *f* = nobody, 33
petit *m,s adj* = little, 3
peu = little, 22
peur *f* = fear, 44
peur (avoir) = to be afraid, 2
peut-être = perhaps; maybe, 32
peux (je) = I can (See *pouvoir*), 8
pièce *f* = room, 10
pied *m* = foot, 20

piéger = to trap, 34
pierre *f* = stone, 19
pire = worse, 26
pleurer = to cry, 10
pleurnicher = to whimper; to snivel, 17
plouf! = splash!, 28
pluie *f* = rain, 27
plus = more, 34
plus loin = farther, 34
plus près (de) = closer, 23
porte *f* = door, 3
poser = to put (down); to place; to ask, 23
poser (se) = to arise, 28
pour = for; to; in order to; so as, 6
pourquoi = why, 23
poursuite *f* = pursuit, 33
pourtant = yet; nevertheless; however, 17
pousser = to push, 12
poussière *f* = dust, 21
pouvoir = to be able to; can, 8
pouvons-nous? = can we?, 16
prendre = to take, 33
près = close (by); near(by), 23
presque = almost; nearly, 20
preuve *f* = proof, 22
proche = close (by), 24
profiter de = to take advantage of, 29
protéger = to protect, 25
provenir de = to come from, 44
puis = then, 20
puisque = since, 12

quand = when, 32
quatre = four, 3
que = that, 15
quelle *f,s adj* = what, 24
quelque chose = something, 10
quelques = a few; some, 46
quelqu'un = someone; somebody, 24
qu'est-ce que c'est? = what is this?, 10
qui = who; that; which, 21

rafale *f* = gust, 25
rapidement = quickly, 29
rappeler = to remind, 25
réagir = to react, 29
recommencer = to start (over) again, 31
reconnaître = to recognize, 28
redoutable = dreadful, 22
redresser (se) = to straighten up, 22
réfléchir = to think; to reflect, 17
regard *m* = gaze; look; eyes, 20
regarder = to look at, 13
regretter = to be sorry, 46
rejoindre = to (re)join; to meet (again), 24
remarquer = to notice, 30
remplir = to fill, 33
rendre compte (se) = to realize, 23
rentrer = to re-enter a place; to go (come) back in, 19
répondre = to answer, 22
réponse *f* = answer; reply, 20
reposer = to lie; to rest, 22
reprendre = to regain; to resume, 24
résonner = to resonate, 25
respirer = to breathe, 34
respirer à fond = to take a deep breath, 26
ressembler à = to resemble; to look like, 14
ressentir = to feel, 28
reste (du) = what's more; besides, 23
rester = to stay, 32
retourner (se) = to turn around, 33
retrouver = to find again; to regain, 22
réussir = to succeed, 30
révéler = to reveal, 28
rien = nothing, 9
rire = to laugh, 8
rire *m* = laugh, 29
rose = pink, 18
rouge = red, 18
ruse *f* = ruse; trick, 32

sa *f,s adj* = his; her, 20

s'agenouiller = to kneel (down), 25

sain *m,s adj* = healthy; sound, 46

sain et sauf = safe and sound (Literal: sound and safe), 46

sans = without, 21

sans doute = no doubt, 31

s'appeler = to be named; to call oneself, 6

s'attendre à = to expect, 33

sauf = except, 13

sauf *m,s adj* = unharmed, 46

sauter = to jump, 33

sautiller = to jump about, 33

sauver = to save, 23

savez (vous) = you know (See *savoir*), 16

savoir = to know, 35

se = oneself; himself; herself; themselves; itself, 6

secouer = to shake, 44

secours! (au) = help!, 44

se fâcher = to get angry, 31

se lever = to get up, 23

semaine *f* = week, 10

sembler = to seem, 27

se moquer de = to make fun of, 25

sentir = to smell, 46

sept = seven, 3

serait (ce) = it would be, 22

se rendre compte = to realize, 23

ses *m,f,pl adj* = his; her, 20

se souvenir de = to remember, 16

s'essuyer = to wipe oneself; to dry oneself, 27

seuil *m* = threshold; doorstep, 44

seule *f,s adj* = alone, 8

si = if; so; such, 12, 28

si = yes (After a negative question), 46

siffler = to whistle, 18

sinon = if not; otherwise, 23

six = six, 3

soigneusement = carefully, 24

soin *m* = care, 24

soldat *m* = soldier, 22

sombre = dark, 10

son *m* = sound, 29

son *m,s adj* = his; her; its, 18

sonore *adj* = resonant, 29

sorte *f* = sort; kind, 19

sortie *f* = exit, 16

sortir = to go out; to get out; to leave, 24

soucieux *m adj* = worried, 19

soudain = suddenly, 17

souffle *m* = breath, 23

souffler = to blow, 23

soupirer = to sigh, 32

sourire = to smile, 22

sourire *m* = smile, 29

sous = under, 22

souvenir de (se) = to remember, 16

s'ouvrir = to open (itself), 19

spectre *m* = ghost; specter, 33

subitement = suddenly, 27

sucette *f* = lollipop, 11

sueur *f* = sweat, 22

suis (je) = I am (See *être*), 1

suit (il) = it follows (See *suivre*), 24

suivant = following, 19

suivre = to follow, 24

sujet *m* = subject, 29

supplier = to beg, 22

sur = on; upon, 10

sûrement = surely, 12

surprenant *m,s adj* = surprising, 23

surtout = especially, 21

tableau *m* = painting, 16

taille *f* = size, 19

tais-toi = be quiet, 19

tant pis = too bad, 19

tard = late, 11

te = you; yourself, 6, 27

tellement = so, 10

témoigner de = to bear witness to; to show, 19

tempête = storm; gale, 29

temps *m* = time; weather, 27

tendre = to hold out; to extend, 21

tenir = to hold, 44

terre *f* = ground; earth, 28

tête *f* = head, 20

tient (il) = he holds (See *tenir*), 44
tirer = to pull, 7
toi = you, 31
tombeau *m* = tomb, 19
tomber = to fall, 12
ton *m,s adj* = your, 18
tonitruante *f,s adj* = thunderous, 44
tonnerre *m* = thunder, 25
tordu *m,s adj* = twisted, 14
totalement = totally, 13
toucher = to touch, 16
touchons = let's touch, 16
toujours = always; forever; still, 30
toupie *f* = top, 23
tour *m* = turn, 25
tour (à mon or à son) = in turn, 30
tourbillon *m* = whirlwind, 24
tourner vers (se) = to turn toward, 21
tous *m,pl* = all, 17
tous les deux = both, 16
tous les jours = every day, 1
tout *m,s adj* = all, 17
tout à coup = suddenly; all of a
    sudden, 11
tout de suite = immediately, 19
toute seule = all alone, 17
traits *m,pl* = features, 44
traverser = to cross, 21
tremper jusqu'aux os (être) = to be
    soaked to the bone (skin), 26
très = very, 2
triste = sad, 27
trois = three, 3
trop = too; too much, 11
trou *m* = hole, 12
trouver = to find, 24
tu = you, 1
tu as raison = you are right, 17
tuer = to kill, 21
tue-tête (crier à) = to shout one's head
    off; to shout or yell at the top of
    one's voice, 30
tu vas bien? = are you all right?, 34

un *m* = a; one, 7
une *f* = a; one, 7
un peu = a little, 34

venir = to come, 24
vent *m* = wind, 18
vent soufflant en tempête = gale force
    wind(s), 25
vers = toward(s), 9
vert *m,s adj* = green, 18
veut (il) = he wants (See *vouloir*), 25
vexer = to hurt; to offend, 22
vide = empty, 13
vie *f* = life, 26
vient (il) = he comes (See *venir*), 24
violet *m,s adj* = purple; violet, 18
visage *m* = face, 20
vite = quickly; quick; fast, 10
vitesse *f* = speed, 21
vivant = living; alive, 14
vlan! (et) = wham!, 23
voici = here is, 22
voie *f* = track; route, 29
voir = to see, 12
vois (je) = I see (See *voir*), 12
voix *f* = voice, 5
vos *m,f,pl adj* = your, 12
voulez-vous? = do you want?, 5
vouloir = to want, 25
vous = you; yourself; yourselves, 1, 6,
    27
voyons (nous) = we see (See *voir*), 12
vrai = true, 28
vraiment = really; truly, 32
vu = saw (See *voir*), 17

y = it; there, 16
y a-t-il? = is there?; are there?, 24
yeux *pl* = eyes, 20

~~ ABOUT THE AUTHOR AND EDITOR ~~

The author is an Indiana University graduate and former medical doctor educated at the Université de Paris, France. She also attended the Sorbonne in Paris and received a Certificat de Phonétique Appliquée à la Langue Française. Having lived and worked in Paris for 13 years, she now has dual nationality. She has most recently become a teacher and writer, using her life experiences in the creation of *The Twisted Doors* series. Dr. Dior is currently using *Les portes tordues* to teach French at the Purdue University Gifted Education Resource Institute in West Lafayette, Indiana.

The book was edited by Dr. Servanne Woodward, native French speaker and holder of a Ph.D. in French from the University of Wisconsin at Madison. Dr. Woodward is currently an associate professor of French at the University of Western Ontario, Canada, and is a specialist in Eighteenth-Century French and professor for Ph.D. candidates.